Collins
English for Work

Hotel & Hospitality English
Mike Seymour

Collins

HarperCollins Publishers
77-85 Fulham Palace Road
Hammersmith
London W6 8JB

First edition 2011

Reprint 10 9 8 7 6 5 4 3 2 1 0

© HarperCollins Publishers 2012

ISBN 978-85-7827-490-0

Published in Brazil by Editora WMF Martins Fontes Ltda by arrangement with HarperCollins Publishers Ltd.

WMF IDIOMAS

uma divisão da Editora WMF Martins Fontes

Collins ® is a registered trademark
of HarperCollins Publishers Limited

www.collinselt.com

A catalogue record for this book is available
from the British Library.

Typeset in India by Aptara

Printed in China by Leo Paper Products Ltd.

All rights reserved. No part of this book may
be reproduced, stored in a retrieval system, or
transmitted in any form or by any means, electronic,
mechanical, photocopying, recording or otherwise,
without the prior permission in writing of the
Publisher. This book is sold subject to the conditions
that it shall not, by way of trade or otherwise,
be lent, re-sold, hired out or otherwise circulated
without the Publisher's prior consent in any form
of binding or cover other than that in which it is
published and without a similar condition including
this condition being imposed on the subsequent
purchaser.

Photographs by Toby Madden
Photographic models: Christina Anastasia, Amy Anzel,
Luke Barron, Tina Chang, Stephen de Martin
Photographs taken on location at Mint Hotel

Introduction

Welcome to Hotel & Hospitality English

This course gives you the English you need to talk to guests – from the moment they arrive at your hotel until the time they check out and you say goodbye.

The 24 units focus on face-to-face communication with guests, plus telephoning and writing emails.

Each unit begins with a conversation for you to listen to and read. The conversation presents the key language. Then there are activities for you to practise the key language including speaking exercises. There is an Answer key at the back of the book.

There are two Audio CDs in the pack. These contain the conversations and speaking activities.

If you see this symbol 🔊, you need to listen to the CD.

We recommend you spend about 45 to 60 minutes on each unit.

In addition, at the back of the book, there are very useful reference sections for you to use and refer to in your day-to-day work.

While you are working through this book, you will see the following symbols after certain words:

[UK] means that the word is more commonly used in British English.
[US] means that the word is more commonly used in American English.

We hope you enjoy using this self-study course. Good luck in your career!

Contents

1	Welcoming guests	6
2	Welcoming a guest with no reservation	10
3	'Difficult' guests	14
4	Looking after guests (1)	18
5	Looking after guests (2)	22
6	Reservation inquiries	26
7	Reservation changes	30
8	Phone calls to reception	34
9	Communication problems	38
10	Guest problems	42
11	At breakfast	46
12	At the bar	50
13	Complaints from guests at the bar	54
14	In the restaurant (1)	58
15	In the restaurant (2)	62
16	In the restaurant (3)	66
17	Housekeeping	70
18	Housekeeping problems	74
19	Room service	78
20	Guest services	82
21	In the business centre	86
22	Recommendations for places to eat	90
23	Checking out	94
24	Problems checking out	98

Resource bank

Answer key / Audio script	102
Key phrases	126
Key words	128
Grammar reference	142
Model emails	150
How do I say ...?	154
On the phone	156

1 Welcoming guests

Checking in guests | Finding out what guests need | Giving guests information

Conversation

1 Sarah works in Reception at the Metro Hotel. She is checking in a guest. Listen to the conversation.

Sarah	**Good afternoon**, madam. **Welcome to the Metro Hotel.**
Guest	Good afternoon. My name's Caroline Brown. I have a reservation.
Sarah	Of course, Ms Brown. One moment, please. Yes, here it is. One double room for three nights.
Guest	That's correct. Could I have a room on a lower floor, please? I don't like using the lift.
Sarah	Is the second floor OK?
Guest	Yes, that's perfect. Thank you.
Sarah	**Could I have your credit card, please?**
Guest	Yes, here's my VISA card.
Sarah	Thank you. You're in Room 209. **Please sign here.** And **would you like a wake-up call?**
Guest	Oh, yes. Could I have a wake-up call at 6.30 tomorrow, please?
Sarah	Of course, 6.30. **Would you like a newspaper?**

Hotel & Hospitality English

Welcoming guests | Unit 1

Guest	Yes, I'd like *The Times* every morning, please. And what time's breakfast?
Sarah	**Breakfast is between 7.00 and 10.30.**
Guest	Thank you.
Sarah	**Enjoy your stay**, Ms Brown.

Language tip

Before Sarah knows the guest's name she calls Ms Brown *madam*. In British English it is polite to call female guests *madam*. In American English *ma'am* is used.

Did you know?

In British English the word is *lift*. In American English it is *elevator*.
The *ground floor* in British English is the *first floor* in American English.

Understanding

2 Listen to the conversation again and answer these questions.

1. Does Ms Brown have a reservation?
2. What kind of room does she ask for?
3. Why does she want this kind of room?
4. What time does she ask for a wake-up call?
5. When does the hotel serve breakfast?

Key phrases

Checking in

Good morning / Good afternoon / Good evening.	Would you like a wake-up call?
Welcome to the Metro Hotel.	Would you like a newspaper?
Could I have your credit card, please?	Breakfast is between ... and ... .
Please sign here.	Enjoy your stay.

Language tip

Sarah calls Caroline Brown 'Ms Brown'. Ms can be used for married or unmarried women.

Hotel & Hospitality English | 7

Practice

3 Put the words in the sentences into the correct order.

1 stay your Enjoy
_____.

2 wake-up like you a call Would
_____?

3 to hotel the Welcome
_____.

4 is 7.00 Breakfast between and 10.30
_____.

5 your have Could I credit card, please
_____?

4 Complete the sentences in this conversation. Then listen to Track 02 to check your answers.

Sarah	Good afternoon, sir. (1) _____ to the Star Hotel.
Guest	Good afternoon. My name's George Melas. I have a (2) _____.
Sarah	Of course, Mr Melas. One (3) _____, please. A single room for two nights?
Guest	Yes, that's right. Could I have a room on a quiet (4) _____, please?
Sarah	I will put you on the top (5) _____. Is that OK?
Guest	Yes, that's great. Thank you.
Sarah	Could I (6) _____ your (7) _____ card, please?
Guest	Here you are.
Sarah	Please (8) _____ here. Thank you.
Guest	Could I have a (9) _____ call at 8 o'clock tomorrow, please?
Sarah	Yes, of course. I hope that you (10) _____ your stay, Mr Melas.
Guest	Thank you.

Hotel & Hospitality English

Welcoming guests | Unit 1

> ### Language tip
>
> When we say the time, we say either *7 o'clock in the morning/evening* or *7 am* (morning) / *7 pm* (evening). We don't say *7 o'clock pm*. If we are not talking about full hours, for example, *10.30*, we don't use the words *o'clock*. We don't say *10.30 o'clock*. We say *ten thirty* or *half past ten*.

Speaking

5 Listen to these times and repeat them.

1 11.30	**3** 10.00	**5** 9.10	**7** 9.50	**9** 3.15
2 7.00	**4** 12.20	**6** 5.45	**8** 1.15	**10** 2.40

6 You are at Reception when a guest arrives. Read the cues given and check in the guest. Play Track 04 and speak after the beep. You start. Then listen to Track 05 to compare your conversation.

You	(*Say hello to guest in a friendly way.*)
Guest	Hello, my name's Yang. I have a reservation for one night.
You	(*Ask for guest's credit card.*)
Guest	Here's my VISA card.
You	(*Ask guest if she wants a wake-up call.*)
Guest	Yes. I would like one at 6 o'clock tomorrow morning, please.
You	(*Confirm time and ask guest if she wants a newspaper in the morning.*)
Guest	Yes. Could I have a *Wall Street Journal*, please?
You	(*Say yes.*)
Guest	What time's breakfast?
You	(*Tell guest 7.00 to 10.30 and wish guest a nice stay in the hotel.*)

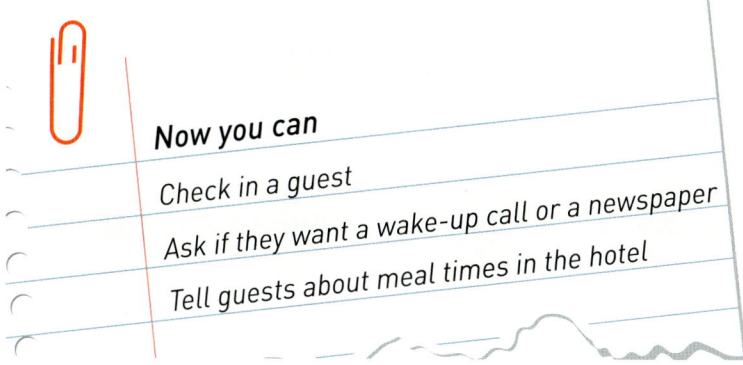

Now you can
Check in a guest
Ask if they want a wake-up call or a newspaper
Tell guests about meal times in the hotel

Hotel & Hospitality English

2 Welcoming a guest with no reservation

Checking in guests | Handling a difficult situation | Saying *No* politely

Conversation

 1 A guest has arrived without a reservation. Sarah is checking him in. Listen to the conversation.

Sarah	Good afternoon, sir. **How can I help you?**
Guest	Hi. I need a room for this evening.
Sarah	**Do you have a reservation?**
Guest	No, I don't. My flight's been delayed until tomorrow evening and I need to stay in the city overnight.
Sarah	**I can offer you our walk-up rate** which is £165 per night for a double room including breakfast.
Guest	That's very expensive. Is that the cheapest rate you have?
Sarah	**I'm afraid so. We're very busy this evening.**
Guest	OK. I'll take it.
Sarah	Fine. ... **Could you fill in this guest registration card for me, please?**
Guest	Can I pay by cheque?

Hotel & Hospitality English

Welcoming a guest with no reservation | Unit 2

Sarah	**I'm afraid not.** Cash or credit card only, I'm afraid. It's hotel policy.
Guest	What time do I have to check out tomorrow?
Sarah	Our usual check-out time is 11 o'clock, sir, but with this rate you can have a late check-out until 2 pm.
Guest	That's great, thanks.

Understanding

2 Listen to the conversation again. Are these statements True or False?

1 The guest's flight has been cancelled. T / F
2 The hotel is very busy this evening. T / F
3 The room costs £165 plus breakfast. T / F
4 Usual check-out time in the hotel is 11 am. T / F
5 The guest can stay in his room until 2 pm. T / F

Key phrases

Checking in a guest without a reservation

How can I help you?	I'm afraid so / not.
Do you have a reservation?	We're very busy this evening / this weekend.
I can offer you … .	Could you fill in this guest registration card for me, please?
Our rack rate / walk-up rate is … .	

Did you know?

The *rack rate* is the standard price a hotel charges for a room. It is the published rate for a room and is used as a basis to calculate any discounts. It is also called the *run of the house* or *walk-up rate*.

Hotel & Hospitality English

Practice

3 Put the words in the sentences into the correct order.

1 have you a reservation Do

   _____?

2 so afraid I'm

   _____.

3 you walk-up our can rate I offer

   _____.

4 busy evening very this We're

   _____.

4 Use the words in the box to complete this guest registration form.

Country code   Nationality   Post code   Signature   Street name   Surname

Title: Mr / Mrs / Ms **(1)** _____: Jones **First name**: Chris

Number / (2) _____: 73 Westbourne Road   **City**: OXFORD

(3) _____: OX3 7GY

Country: UK   **(4)** _____: British

Phone No.: **(5)** (_____) +44 **(Area code)** 1607
(Phone number) 580 4411

E-Mail address: CJones@freetel.com
Car Registration No.: SXY 3LQ

Date and (6) _____: *CJones*

Did you know?

In British English it is *post code*. In American English it is *zip code*.

Language tip

Use the phrase *I'm afraid* to soften messages that contain bad or unhelpful news and to make them sound more polite. For example: *Can I pay by cheque? – I'm afraid you can't pay by cheque. Is the restaurant closed? – I'm afraid the restaurant is closed.* It is like saying sorry in advance. You can also use the short forms *I'm afraid not* and *I'm afraid so* as replies.

Speaking

5 Practise softening your language. Add *I'm afraid* to make these sentences sound more polite. Listen to Track 07 to compare your answers.

1 The hotel doesn't accept cheques.
Your version: _____

2 We have no vacancies this evening.
Your version: _____

3 You have to check out at noon.
Your version: _____

4 That's the best rate I can offer you, sir.
Your version: _____

6 Reply to these questions from guests using *I'm afraid so* or *I'm afraid not*. Listen to Track 08 to compare your answers.

1 **Guest** My room is very small. Can you upgrade it to a suite?
Your reply _____

2 **Guest** Do I really have to check out of my room by 12.00?
Your reply _____

3 **Guest** Is the bar open now?
Your reply _____

4 **Guest** Is that charge for phone calls really correct?
Your reply _____

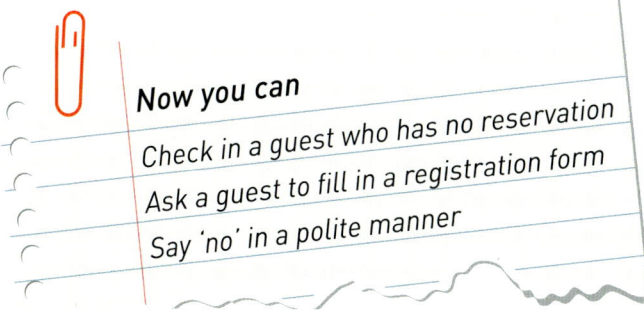

Now you can
Check in a guest who has no reservation
Ask a guest to fill in a registration form
Say 'no' in a polite manner

3 'Difficult' guests

Explaining things | Finding solutions to problems | Making suggestions

Conversation

09
CD1

1 Sarah is checking in a guest who has arrived early. Listen to the conversation.

Sarah	Good morning, sir. How are you today?
Guest	Fine, thank you. I have a reservation in the name of Lopez.
Sarah	Mr Diego Lopez?
Guest	Yes, that's right.
Sarah	You're staying with us for two nights.
Guest	Yes, that's correct.
Sarah	**I'm sorry**, Mr Lopez. **Your room isn't quite ready yet. Normally our check-in is from** 2 pm.
Guest	Yes, I know that but my flight arrived early.
Sarah	**I'm sorry but Housekeeping are still cleaning your room.**
Guest	That's not very good. What do you suggest I do?
Sarah	Well, **you're welcome to store** your luggage with us. **May I suggest** you have a cup of coffee in the restaurant? When your room's ready, I'll come and get you. Is that OK?

14 | Hotel & Hospitality English

'Difficult' guests | Unit 3

Guest	OK, but how long will that be?
Sarah	**I'll ask Housekeeping to do your room as quickly as possible.**
Guest	Thank you. I'd appreciate it. I want to freshen up and get changed before my meeting. How do I get to the restaurant?
Sarah	Just go around the corner to your right, sir.

Did you know?

Baggage is another word for *luggage*. Suitcases, rucksacks and holdalls are types of baggage.

Understanding

2 Listen to the conversation again and answer these questions.

1. Does Mr Lopez have a reservation?
2. Why can't Mr Lopez check in?
3. What time is the usual check-in time?
4. What two things does Sarah suggest?
5. Why does Mr Lopez want to check in as soon as possible?

Key phrases

Dealing with 'difficult' guests

I'm sorry your room isn't quite ready yet.	You're welcome to do / store / wait / sit … .
Normally our check-in is from … .	May I suggest … ?
I'm sorry but Housekeeping are still cleaning the room.	I'll ask Housekeeping to do / clean / prepare your room as quickly as possible.

Language tip

Notice how we use *not quite*. Sarah says that *the room isn't quite ready* to indicate it is *almost* ready. She could also say *Housekeeping haven't quite finished cleaning the room*.

Practice

3 Choose the right word to complete the sentences.

1 We would be glad to _____ your luggage while you are waiting.
   store   sell   lose
2 May I _____ you have a drink in the bar while you are waiting?
   suggest   offer   ask
3 I'm sorry, sir. Your room isn't _____ ready yet.
   quite   totally   fully
4 When your room is ready, I'll come and _____ you.
   send   get   check
5 Our normal check-in time is _____ 2 pm.
   from   in   on
6 You're staying with us _____ two nights.
   for   about   over
7 The coffee shop is just around the corner _____ your right.
   to   at   in

4 Complete the sentences with words from the box.

| afraid   cleaning   suggest   welcome   ready   Normally   get |

1 _____ our check-in is from 2 pm.
2 You're _____ to store your luggage.
3 Your room isn't quite _____ yet.
4 May I _____ you wait in the restaurant?
5 Housekeeping are still _____ your room.
6 I'll come and _____ you when your room's ready.
7 I'm _____ your room isn't ready yet, sir.

Language tip

In English we use *I'm sorry* to apologize, even when something isn't our fault or responsibility! We can also add *very* to make the apology stronger, for example, *I'm very sorry*.

'Difficult' guests | Unit 3

Speaking

5 Practise apologizing. Add *I'm sorry* to these sentences. Listen to Track 10 to compare your answers.

1 Your room isn't ready yet, sir.
Your version: _____

2 You're too early to check in, sir.
Your version: _____

3 Housekeeping are still cleaning the rooms, madam.
Your version: _____

4 I don't have any rooms ready at the moment.
Your version: _____

6 A guest has arrived too early to check in. Play Track 11 and speak after the beep. You start. Then listen to Track 12 to compare your conversation.

You	(*Greet the guest.*)
Guest	Good morning. I have a reservation for tonight. My name's Jens Weiler.
You	(*You have been expecting Mr Weiler.*)
Guest	When can I check in?
You	(*Check-in is from 2 pm.*)
Guest	But I have a very heavy suitcase.
You	(*Offer to store his suitcase.*)
Guest	And what should I do until my room is ready?
You	(*Suggest a coffee in the coffee shop.*)
Guest	And where is the coffee shop?
You	(*Around the corner on the left.*)

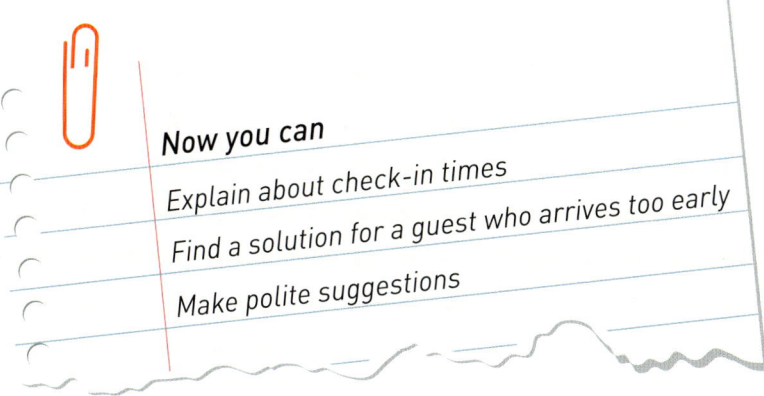

Now you can

Explain about check-in times

Find a solution for a guest who arrives too early

Make polite suggestions

Hotel & Hospitality English

4 Looking after guests (1)

Offering to help | Giving simple directions | Explaining things

Conversation

1 Simon works as a concierge in Guest Services. Listen to the conversation.

13
CD1

Simon	Good evening, madam. **Can I help you?**
Guest	Yes. I've just checked in and I don't have any local currency. Is there an ATM in the hotel?
Simon	Sorry, madam, **I didn't quite catch that**. Is there *a what* in the hotel?
Guest	An ATM, a cash machine – somewhere I can take out some money?
Simon	Ah, now I understand. I'm sorry, madam, I'm afraid there isn't a cash machine in the hotel but there are lots of banks on Maple Street, which isn't far away.
Guest	Could you show me where it is?
Simon	Sure. **Let me give you a map of the city.** The hotel is here. Look, I'll circle it for you. Maple Street **is about five minutes' walk away**.
Guest	Could you show me how to get there?
Simon	Of course. **Turn right out of the hotel. Walk along the street and turn left at the traffic lights.** Walk along Hope Street and then turn right onto Maple Street. There are lots of banks there with cash machines.
Guest	Thank you very much.
Simon	My pleasure, madam.

18 | Hotel & Hospitality English

Looking after guests (1) | Unit 4

Language tip

Simon says *My pleasure*. You can also say *You're welcome* or, in a more informal situation, *No problem.*

Did you know?

ATM stands for *Automated Teller Machine* but we just say *ATM*. Another word for *cash machine* is *cashpoint* or *cash dispenser*. Some people refer to *cash machines* as a *hole in the wall*!

Understanding

2 Listen to the conversation again and answer these questions.
   1 When did the guest arrive?
   2 What does the guest need to find?
   3 What did Simon not understand?
   4 How far away is Maple Street?

Key phrases

Helping guests and giving directions

Can I help you?	Turn left / right out of the hotel.
I didn't quite catch that.	Walk along ... .
Let me give you ... (a map).	It's about ... minutes / metres / miles away.

Hotel & Hospitality English | 19

> **Language tip**
>
> Note that Simon says *Sorry, madam, I didn't quite catch that* when he doesn't understand what the guest says and wants. This is a friendly and informal way of saying that you haven't heard or understood something.

Practice

3 Use the words in the box to complete the sentences.

catch circle map pleasure turn

1 Sorry, madam, I didn't quite _____ what you said.
2 When you get to the end of the street _____ left into Rothwell Lane.
3 Let me show you where we are on this _____ .
4 My _____ , madam.
5 I'll _____ the street on this map for you.

4 Look at the map and complete the directions.

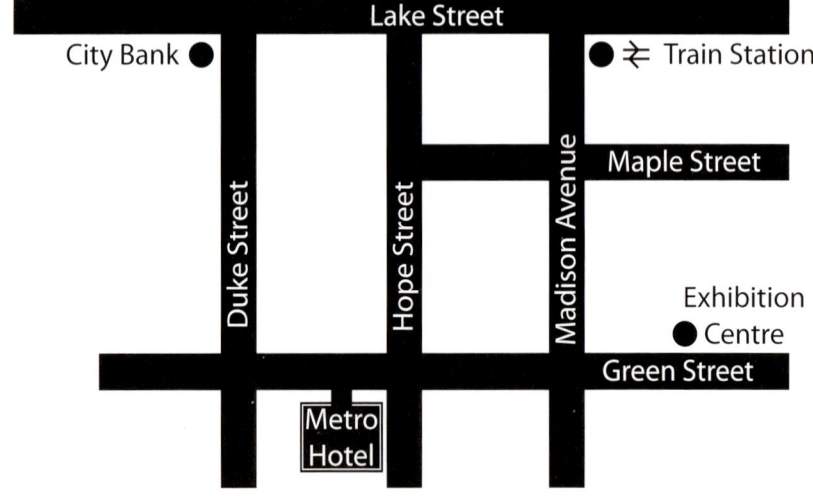

1 **Guest** Can you tell me how to get to the City Bank?
   You Yes, of course. Turn (1) _____ out of the hotel and walk along Green Street. Turn (2) _____ onto Duke Street. The City Bank is on the (3) _____ .

2 **Guest** Can you tell me how to get to the Exhibition Centre?
   You Yes, of course. Turn (4) _____ out of the hotel and walk along Green Street. The Exhibition Centre is on the (5) _____ .

Looking after guests (1) | Unit 4

Speaking

5 Practise showing you do not understand something. Use sorry *I didn't quite catch ...* . Listen to Track 14 to compare your answers.

Guest	Hello. My name is Monika Schl.... I have a meeting at ten o'clock with one of your guests.
You	_____ .
Guest	I have to go to an office on R... Lane.
You	_____ .
Guest	My booking reference is MH276....
You	_____ .

6 A guest wants to know how to get to the train station. Use the map on the opposite page to explain how to get there. Play Track 15 and speak after the beep. You start. Then listen to Track 16 to compare your conversation.

You	*(It's 6 pm. Greet the guest.)*
Guest	I need to get to the train station. Can you tell me where it is?
You	*(Give the guest a map; point to the hotel; offer to circle it.)*
Guest	Thank you very much.
You	*(Tell the guest the train station is 10 minutes' walk away.)*
Guest	OK.
You	*(Give the guest directions.)*
Guest	That's very clear. Thank you very much.
You	*(Respond politely.)*

Now you can

Offer guests information

Tell guests how to get to places

Explain things clearly

Hotel & Hospitality English

5 Looking after guests (2)

Organizing transport | Giving information to guests | Agreeing to do something

Conversations

1 Simon is at the Guest Services desk. Listen to the two conversations.

A

Simon	Hello madam. Can I help you?
Guest	Yes. Can you order me a taxi for later today, please?
Simon	Sure, madam, **what time do you need it?**
Guest	I have to be at the Exhibition Centre at 10 am.
Simon	OK. **I'll order you a taxi for** a quarter to ten. What's your room number, please?
Guest	Room 1002 – Mrs Hepworth.
Simon	Fine, Mrs Hepworth. **I'll call your room when your taxi arrives.**
Guest	Thank you very much.
Simon	You're welcome. **Have a nice day.**

Hotel & Hospitality English

B

Simon	Good morning, sir, how can I help you?
Guest	Hello, does the hotel have a business centre?
Simon	Yes, but I'm afraid there's a conference in the business centre today, sir, but **there are three computers with Internet access in the lobby** and **all rooms have free Wi-Fi.**
Guest	I need to send a fax abroad.
Simon	Reception will be happy to do that for you. We charge 75 pence per page.
Guest	OK. And I'm expecting a fax. When it arrives, can you bring it up to my room, please?
Simon	Of course. **We'll do that as soon as it arrives.** Can you tell me your room number, please?
Guest	532. My name's Smith.
Simon	Thank you.

Understanding

2 Listen to the conversations again and answer these questions.

1. What does Mrs Hepworth ask Simon to do?
2. Where does Mrs Hepworth have to go?
3. When does Mrs Hepworth have to be there?
4. What does Mr Smith want to do?
5. Which department in the hotel will help him?
6. How much will it cost?

Key phrases

Helping guests

What time do you need …?	*There are three computers with Internet access in the lobby.*
I'll order you a taxi for …	
I'll call your room when your taxi arrives.	*All rooms have free Wi-Fi.*
Have a nice day.	*We'll do that as soon as it arrives.*

Did you know?

Cab is another word for *taxi*.

Practice

3 Match the two halves of the sentences.

1 How can I
2 What time
3 As soon as the fax arrives,
4 I'll order you a taxi
5 I'll call your room

A we'll bring it to your room.
B when the taxi arrives.
C help you?
D do you need a taxi?
E for a quarter to ten.

4 In Conversation A, Mrs Hepworth asked Simon to order her a taxi. Simon now calls her room to tell her that the taxi is there. Put the sentences into the correct order. The first one has been done for you. Listen to Track 18 to check your answer.

1	Guest:	Hello? Jill Hepworth speaking.
	Guest:	Good morning.
	Guest:	Please tell the driver I'll be down in five minutes.
	Simon:	Very good, madam. I'll tell the taxi driver that you'll be here soon.
	Simon:	Good morning, Mrs Hepworth. This is Simon from Guest Services.
	Simon:	I'm calling to let you know that your taxi has arrived.

Language tip

When we promise or agree to do something for somebody we use *will*, for example, *I'll (I will) order you a taxi for 9.30* or *They'll (They will) organize it for you.*

Hotel & Hospitality English

Looking after guests (2) | Unit 5

Speaking

5 You work at the Guest Services desk. What do you say in these two situations? Play Track 19 and speak after the beep. You start. Then listen to the model conversations on Track 20.

A **You** *(Greet the guest.)*
Guest Yes, I have a question. Does the hotel have a swimming pool?
You *(Apologize and tell the guest there is no pool.)*
Guest Oh. What a pity. Never mind.
You *(Apologize.)*

B **You** *(Greet the guest.)*
Guest Hello. Could you order me a taxi for later, please?
You *(Ask the guest what time she needs the taxi.)*
Guest I need it at noon.
You *(Tell the guest you will call her room when it arrives.)*
Guest Thank you.
You *(Respond politely.)*

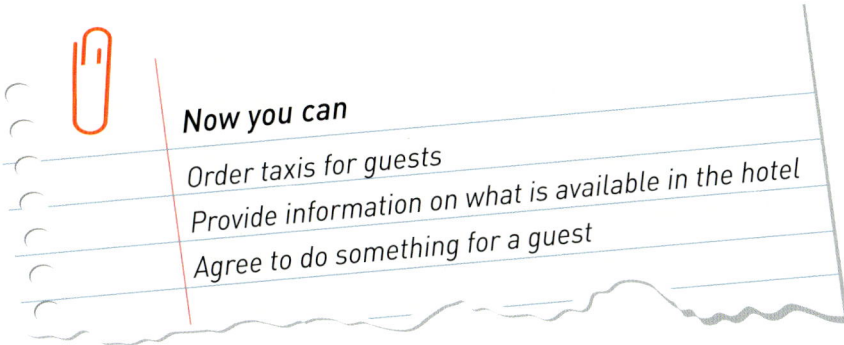

Now you can
Order taxis for guests
Provide information on what is available in the hotel
Agree to do something for a guest

Hotel & Hospitality English | 25

6 Reservation inquiries

Handling reservation inquiries | Taking reservations | Taking credit card details

Conversation

 1 Sarah is at the front desk. She is on the phone. Listen to her conversation.

21
CD1

Sarah	Good morning, Metro Hotel.
Caller	Hello, could I speak to somebody in Reservations, please?
Sarah	Speaking. How can I help you, sir?
Caller	I want to check availability for later this year. I need two rooms for two nights on December 5th.
Sarah	**Let me check**, sir. .... **Yes, we still have availability.**
Caller	What's the best rate you can offer?
Sarah	**I can offer you** our promotional weekend rate of £119 per room per night, bed and breakfast.
Caller	That sounds great. Please reserve two double rooms for me.
Sarah	Of course, sir. Could you give me your name, please?
Caller	It's Leach, Michael Leach.
Sarah	Is that L-E-A-C-H?
Caller	Yes, that's right.
Sarah	Mr Leach, **could you give me a credit card number? I need it to guarantee the reservation.**

Hotel & Hospitality English

Reservation inquiries | Unit 6

Caller	Yes. It's a Mastercard and the number is 8192 5212 6232 9965.
Sarah	I'll just repeat that: 8192 5212 6232 9965.
Caller	That's correct.
Sarah	**Could you tell me the expiry date, please?**
Caller	March 2013.
Sarah	Thank you, Mr Leach. Your reservation number is MH374XY. **We look forward to seeing you in December.** Goodbye.
Caller	Goodbye.

Language tip

Sarah says *Speaking* when the caller asks to speak to someone in Reservations. She means *You are speaking to someone in Reservations.*

You can also use *Speaking* if you answer the telephone and the caller asks to speak to you but doesn't recognize your voice.

Understanding

2 Listen to the conversation again and answer these questions.

1. When does the caller want to stay in the hotel?
2. How much will the room cost?
3. Is the price for bed and breakfast or room only?
4. Is the price per person or per room?
5. Why does Sarah ask for a credit card number?
6. When does the caller's credit card expire?

Key phrases

Reservations inquiries

Let me check.	*I need it to guarantee the reservation.*
Yes, we (still) have availability.	*Could you tell me the expiry date, please?*
I can offer you … .	*We look forward to seeing you in December.*
Could you give me a credit card number?	

Hotel & Hospitality English | 27

Did you know?

In British English it is the *expiry date* of a credit card. In American English you can use the *expiration date*.

In American English it is always a *reservation*. In British English you can also use a *booking*.

Practice

3 Rearrange these words to make complete sentences.

1 check me Let
_____.

2 reservation it need I to the guarantee
_____.

3 tell you me Could date the expiry please
_____?

4 forward you in seeing look to We December
_____.

Language tip

When you repeat back a credit card number to a customer, group the numbers in blocks of four, for example, 4410 pause 4601 pause 7510 pause 5147. In British English, it is more common to say *double four* rather than *four four*, when the same number is repeated. Use *oh* or *zero* for 0.

Reservation inquiries | Unit 6

Speaking

4 Listen to these numbers and repeat them.
1. 5972 6226 2672 3508
2. 2700 6365 6752 8748
3. 2237 3463 7362 7497

5 You are at Reception when the phone rings. Read the cues given to help you deal with the inquiry. Play Track 23 and speak after the beep. You start. Then listen to Track 24 to compare your conversation.

You	(*Answer the phone politely.*)
Caller	Good morning. I'd like to reserve a single room for January 5th, please.
You	(*Say you have availability.*)
Caller	How much will it cost?
You	(*Tell the caller your best rate is £140 per night.*)
Caller	Does that include breakfast?
You	(*Politely tell caller that it's room only.*)
Caller	OK. I'll take it.
You	(*Ask for caller's name and credit card details to confirm the reservation.*)
Caller	It's Gardiner. J Gardiner. My VISA card number is 3412 5679 3451 6012, expiry date 10/14.
You	(*Thank the caller and give them the reservation number MH435XY and end conversation politely.*)
Caller	Goodbye.

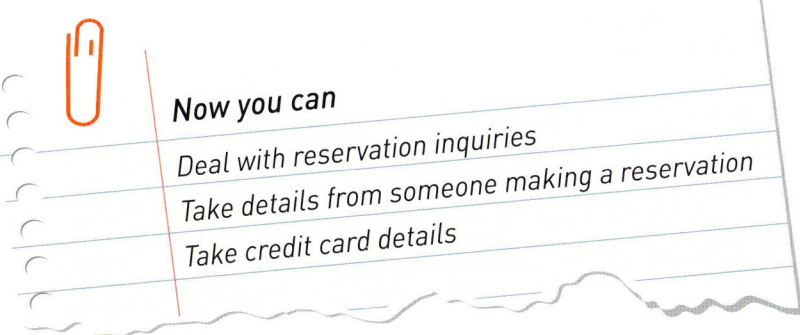

Now you can
Deal with reservation inquiries
Take details from someone making a reservation
Take credit card details

Hotel & Hospitality English

7 Reservation changes

Changing reservations | Cancelling reservations | Confirming cancellations

Conversations

1 Sarah is at the front desk. She is on the phone. Listen to her conversations.

A

Sarah	Good morning, Metro Hotel, Sarah speaking.
Caller	Hello, my name is Michael Leach. I'd like to change a reservation, please.
Sarah	Certainly, Mr Leach. Do you have the reservation number?
Caller	Yes, it's MH374XY.
Sarah	One moment, please. Your reservation is for two rooms for two nights, arriving on December 5th.
Caller	Yes, that's correct. Now we need two rooms for three nights.
Sarah	Fine, Mr Leach. **I've changed that for you.** Your reservation number is the same.
Caller	Thank you.
Sarah	Goodbye.
Caller	Bye.

Hotel & Hospitality English

Reservation changes | Unit 7

B

Sarah	Metro Hotel, Good afternoon.
Caller	Hi, I need to cancel my reservation for next Tuesday, March 6th. Can you help me with that?
Sarah	Of course. **Could you tell me your name and the reservation number, please?**
Caller	It's Mrs Chen and the reservation number is MH374ET.
Sarah	Mrs Chen, that's fine, **I've cancelled your reservation for you.**
Caller	That's good.
Sarah	**There's no cancellation charge because you've cancelled within our 48-hour cancellation deadline.**
Caller	Good.
Sarah	**Would you like me to send you a confirmation email?**
Caller	Yes, please. Thank you and goodbye.
Sarah	Goodbye.

Understanding

2 Listen to the calls again and answer these questions.

1 What change does the caller in Conversation A want to make?
2 Can Sarah make the change?
3 Does the caller in B pay a cancellation charge?
4 When is the deadline for cancelling reservations free of charge?
5 How does Sarah confirm the cancellation in B?

Key phrases

Changing and cancelling reservations

Could you tell me your name and the reservation number, please?	*I've cancelled your reservation for you.*
I've changed that [the reservation] for you.	*There's no cancellation charge.*
Would you like me to send you a confirmation email?	*You've cancelled within / outside the cancellation deadline.*

Practice

3 Use the words in the box to complete Sarah's email to Mrs Chen.

> charge   cancelled   forward   reservation   confirmation   there

---

To: lindachen@freenet.com
Cc: guestservices@metrohotels.com

Dear Mrs Chen

Further to our conversation earlier this afternoon, this is (1) _____ that I have (2) _____ your (3) _____ for March 6th. I can also confirm that (4) _____ is no cancellation (5) _____.

We look (6) _____ to seeing you in the future.

Best regards
Sarah Bray
Metrohotels

Language tip

Make polite offers with *Would you like me to ...?* or, in British English, *Shall I ...?* For example, *Would you like me to send you a confirmation email?* or *Shall I ask someone to carry your bags up to your room?*

Did you know?

Nowadays many hotels offer cheaper advance purchase rates, which cannot be changed or cancelled. The cost of the hotel room is charged to your credit card when you make the reservation rather than when you check out.

32 | Hotel & Hospitality English

Reservation changes | Unit 7

Speaking

4 Listen to these dates and repeat them.

1 January 1st	4 April 5th	7 July 20th	10 October 23rd
2 February 2nd	5 May 10th	8 August 21st	11 November 30th
3 March 3rd	6 June 16th	9 September 22nd	12 December 31st

5 You are at Reception when the phone rings. Read the cues given to help you deal with the caller, Mr Jackson, who has a reservation for February 12th. Play Track 27 and speak after the beep. You start. Then listen to Track 28 to compare your conversation.

You	(Answer phone politely.)
Caller	Good morning. I need to cancel a reservation, please.
You	(Ask for reservation number.)
Caller	The reservation number is MF264FK.
You	(Check caller's name and the dates of the stay.)
Caller	Yes, that's correct.
You	(Tell caller that's fine and the room is cancelled.)
Caller	Will there be any charge?
You	(Tell caller no.)
Caller	That's good. Can you send a confirmation email?
You	(Say yes and end call politely.)
Caller	Goodbye.

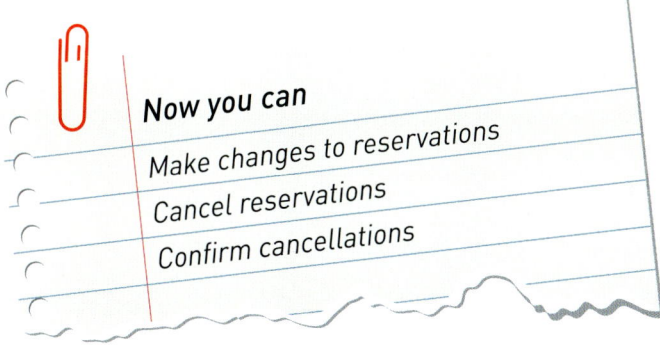

Now you can
Make changes to reservations
Cancel reservations
Confirm cancellations

Hotel & Hospitality English | 33

8 Phone calls to reception

Transferring calls within the hotel | Dealing with guests' problems

Conversations

1 Sarah is at Reception. Listen to her three phone conversations.

29 CD1

A
Sarah	Hello, Reception, Sarah speaking.
Caller	This is Ahmed Tahir in Room 483. I'd like to reserve a table for dinner at 8 pm, please.
Sarah	Certainly, **I'll put you through to** the restaurant.
Caller	Thank you.
Sarah	**Please hold the line.** It's ringing for you now.

B
Sarah	Good morning, Reception, Sarah speaking.
Caller	Hello, this is Caroline Brown in Room 469. The air conditioning isn't working. Can you do anything about it?
Sarah	**I'm very sorry about that. I'll send up someone from Maintenance.**
Caller	How long will that take?
Sarah	We'll be as quick as we can, madam.
Caller	OK. Thank you. Bye.

Hotel & Hospitality English

Phone calls to reception | Unit 8

C

Sarah	Metro Hotel, Sarah speaking.
Caller	Hi, my colleague, Ian Diamond, is staying with you. Can you tell me which room he's staying in, please?
Sarah	**I'm afraid I can't give out our guests' room numbers.**
Caller	Ah!
Sarah	But I can put you through to Mr Diamond's room. Would you like me to do that?
Caller	Yes, please.
Sarah	Hold the line. ... I'm sorry, sir. Mr Diamond isn't in his room. **Would you like to leave a message?**
Caller	No, thanks. I'll try again later.

Did you know?

Many UK and US hotels do not have a thirteenth floor because the number 13 is considered unlucky. What numbers are lucky and unlucky in your culture?

Understanding

2 Listen to the phone calls again and answer these questions.

1. In which call is the caller phoning from outside the hotel, A, B or C?
2. In which call does the caller want to speak to another department of the hotel, A, B or C?
3. In which call does the caller want to speak to a guest, A, B or C?
4. In which call does the caller have a problem, A, B or C?

Key phrases

Answering a front-of-house call

I'll put you through to	*I'm afraid I can't give out our guests' room numbers.*
Please hold the line.	
I'm very sorry about that.	*Would you like to leave a message?*
I'll send up someone from [Maintenance].	

Hotel & Hospitality English

Practice

3 Put the words in the sentences into the correct order.

1 line the Please hold
   _____.

2 I'm room give I can't out our guests' numbers afraid
   _____.

3 restaurant I'll through put to you the now
   _____.

4 Housekeeping send someone from up I'll
   _____.

5 very that sorry about I'm
   _____.

6 Would leave like a you message to
   _____?

4 Number the sentences in the phone conversation in the correct order. The first one is given for you. Then listen to check your answers.

1	Sarah:	Good morning, Metro Hotel, Sarah speaking. How can I help you?
	Mr Novak:	Yes, my name is Novak and I've reserved a double room for Saturday September 18th for two nights.
	Mr Novak:	Yes, that's correct.
	Sarah:	Fine, Mr Novak. I've found your reservation. It is confirmed and your reservation number is MH434CW.
	Sarah:	I'm sorry, Reservations seems to be busy. No one's answering. Could you give me your name?
	Mr Novak:	Good morning. I'm calling to reconfirm a reservation but I've lost my reservation number.
	Sarah:	Is that Mr Jan Novak?
	Mr Novak:	Thank you.
	Sarah:	Hold the line, please. I'll put you through to Reservations.
	Sarah:	Thank you. Goodbye.

Language tip

When you talk about hotel room numbers, say the digits individually rather than as a whole number, for example for Room 409 say *Room four oh nine* not *Room four hundred and nine*.

In a very big hotel, with more than nine floors, you will have room numbers like 1017. In this case, say *Room ten seventeen* not *Room one thousand and seventeen*.

Phone calls to reception | Unit 8

Speaking

5 Listen to these room numbers and repeat them.

1 112   2 608   3 231   4 1142   5 1206

6 You are working at Reception. Read the cues given to help you deal with the guest's question or problem. Play Track 32 and speak after the beep. You start. Then listen to the model answers on Track 33.

A
You (Say good morning and your name.)
Caller I want to make a reservation, please.
You (Put them through to Reservations.)
Caller Thank you.
You (Tell the guest it is ringing.)

B
You (Say good evening and your name.)
Caller Hello. This is Mr Strong in Room 201. We need some more towels.
You (Say what you will do.)
Caller Thank you. How long will that take?
You (Say it will be five minutes.)

C
You (Say good afternoon and your name.)
Caller Good afternoon. Can you give me Ian Diamond's room number, please?
You (Say you can't politely but offer to put the caller through to his room.)
Caller Yes, please.
Ian Diamond Hello, Ian Diamond speaking.

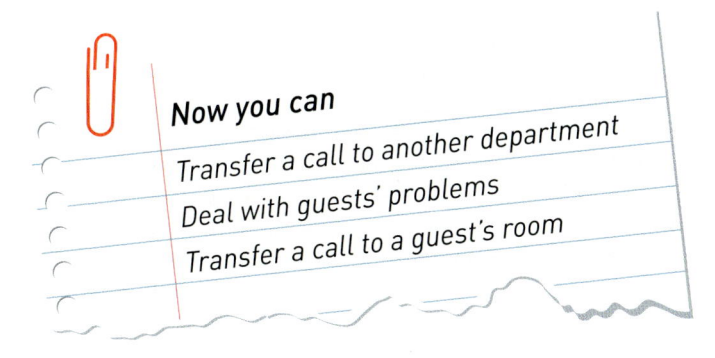

Now you can
- Transfer a call to another department
- Deal with guests' problems
- Transfer a call to a guest's room

Hotel & Hospitality English

9 Communication problems

Dealing with a bad phone line | Confirming details | Making information clear

Conversations

1 Sarah is at the front desk but having some communication problems. Listen to her phone calls.

A

Sarah	Good morning, Metro Hotel. Sarah speaking.
Guest	Good morning. This is Rog … .
Sarah	I'm sorry, sir. **It's a very bad line. I didn't quite catch your name. Could you repeat that?**
Guest	This is Rog … . I want to … .
Sarah	I'm sorry, sir. I can't hear you properly. **Could you possibly call back?**

Guest calls back

Sarah	Good morning, Metro Hotel. Sarah speaking.
Guest	Good morning. This is Roger Dawson. I called a minute ago.
Sarah	Oh hello, Mr Dawson. Yes, that's better. How can I help?
Guest	I'd like to speak to Mr Diamond in Room 721, please.
Sarah	One moment, I'll put you through.

Hotel & Hospitality English

Communication problems | Unit 9

B	Sarah	Good morning, Metro Hotel. Sarah speaking.
	Guest	Hello. I'm calling about a reservation I made last week.
	Sarah	Do you have the reservation number?
	Guest	Yes it's MH4287JM, no, sorry, I mean JN.
	Sarah	I'm sorry. I didn't quite catch the last two letters. **Would you mind repeating the number?**
	Guest	It's MH4287JN.
	Sarah	Sorry, madam. **Is that M for Mike or N for November?**
	Guest	N for November.
	Sarah	Thank you. **Let me just read that back to you**: that's MH4287JN. Reservation for Mrs Harris... .

Did you know?

In American English *Z* is pronounced *zee*. In British English *Z* is pronounced *zed*.

Understanding

2 Listen to the calls again and answer these questions.
  1 In call A, why can't Sarah understand Roger Dawson?
  2 When Roger Dawson calls back, what does he want?
  3 In call B, which information does Sarah have problems with?
  4 What are the correct last two letters of Mrs Harris' reservation number?

Key phrases

Communication problems

It's a very bad line.	Would you mind repeating ... ?
I didn't quite catch your name.	Is that M for Mike or N for November?
Could you repeat that?	Let me (just) read that back to you.
Could you possibly call back?	

Language tip

Use the phrase *Would you mind* + verb + *ing*, for example, *Would you mind spelling your name?* to sound very polite when you ask someone to do something.

Practice

3 Choose the correct verb forms in these sentences.

1 Would you mind **to spell / spelling** your name for me?
2 Could you **repeat / repeating** that for me?
3 I'm sorry. I didn't quite **catch / to catch** what you said.
4 Could you possibly **calling / call** back?
5 One moment, **I'll put / I put** you through.
6 Let me **reading / read** that back to you.

Speaking

4 Use the structure *Would you mind* + verb + *ing* to make these requests very polite. Use the verb in **bold**. Then listen to Track 35 to compare your answers.

1 Please **tell** me your name.
   _____

2 Please **spell** that for me.
   _____

3 Please **repeat** the last three numbers.
   _____

4 Please **call** back later.
   _____

5 Please **use** a different phone.
   _____

Communication problems | Unit 9

5 Practise spelling these names and reservation references. Use the aviation alphabet on page 157 to help you. Then listen to Track 36 to compare your answers.

Example
Martin Herles, Booking Reference MH432ZY
Martin: M for Mike, A for Alpha, R for Romeo, T for Tango, I for India, N for November ...
Booking Reference is: M for Mike, H for Hotel, 4, 3, 2, Z for Zulu and Y for Yankee.

1 Omar Ali, Booking Reference MH965PW
2 Gerry McDonnell, Booking Reference MH732GV
3 Tanya Koshkina, Booking Reference MH645JQ
4 Claire Birkel, Booking Reference MH152SO

6 You are at Reception when you get a call on a bad line. Read the cues given to help you deal with the situation. Play Track 37 and speak after the beep. You start. Then listen to Track 38 to compare your conversation.

You	(*Answer the phone politely.*)
Caller	Good morning. My name is Mi ... . I want to ... .
You	(*Politely tell caller that you can't understand her and ask her to repeat her name.*)
Caller	My name is Michelle ... . I want to ca ... .
You	(*Tell caller you still can't understand her and ask her to call back.*)
Caller	Hello. My name is Michelle Williams and I want to cancel a table for dinner.
You	(*Tell caller that's much better and you will put her through to the restaurant.*)
Caller	Thanks.
You	(*Say it is ringing.*)

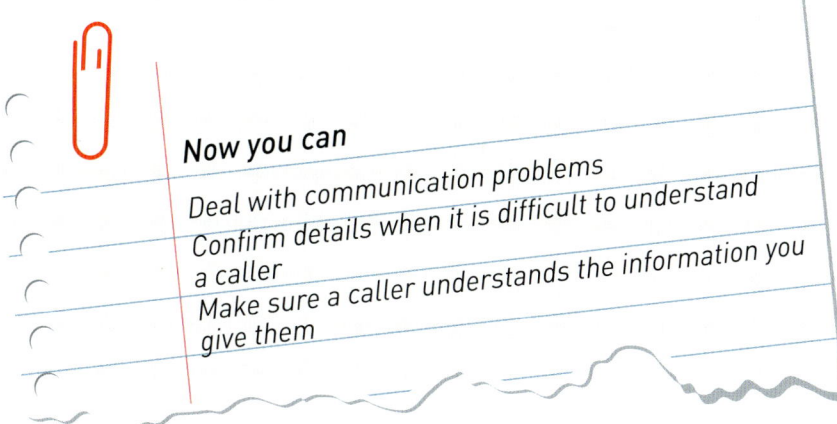

Now you can
Deal with communication problems
Confirm details when it is difficult to understand a caller
Make sure a caller understands the information you give them

10 Guest problems

Handling guest complaints | Solving problems | Moving guests to a new room

Conversations

1 Sarah is at the front desk and has a problem that needs the help of one of her colleagues. Listen to her phone calls.

A

Sarah	Good afternoon, Reception, Sarah speaking. How can I help you?
Guest	Hello. I have a complaint. I've just checked into Room 855 and it smells of smoke.
Sarah	**I'm very sorry to hear that**, madam. **Please accept my apologies.**
Guest	It's horrible.
Sarah	Yes, some guests unfortunately ignore the *No Smoking* signs.
Guest	Well, what are you going to do about it?
Sarah	Don't worry, I'll find you another room immediately. Please wait in your room. **I'll send somebody up to** collect your bags and move you to another room.
Guest	Thank you.
Sarah	**I can offer you a superior room** on a higher floor with a view over the city. **Would that be acceptable?**
Guest	That sounds fine. Thank you very much.

Hotel & Hospitality English

Guest problems | Unit 10

B	Simon	Good afternoon, Guest Services. Simon speaking.
	Sarah	Simon, **this is Sarah**. Please go up to Room 855 ASAP, collect the guest's luggage and move her to Room 1002. She says the room smells of smoke. And tell her we will send up a bottle of wine on the house. Thanks.
	Simon	OK, Sarah, will do.

Did you know?

When we use the abbreviation *ASAP* or *asap*, which stands for *as soon as possible*, we usually say the letters separately, like this A – S – A – P. This is quite informal.

Understanding

2 Listen to the conversations again and decide if these statements are True or False.

1 The guest says that Room 1002 smells of smoke. T / F
2 Sarah will move the unhappy guest to a better room. T / F
3 Sarah tells the unhappy guest to come back down to Reception. T / F
4 Sarah plans to give the unhappy guest a free bottle of wine. T / F
5 The guest is happy with Sarah's solution to the problem. T / F

Key phrases

Handling problems

I'm (very) sorry to hear that.	*I can offer you a superior room.*
Please accept my apologies.	*Would that be acceptable?*
I'll send somebody up to … .	*This is (Sarah).*

Hotel & Hospitality English

Practice

3 Put the words in the sentences into the correct order.

1 accept my apologies Please
   _____.

2 up I'll your send to collect bags somebody
   _____.

3 be that acceptable Would
   _____?

4 offer a room superior you I can
   _____.

4 The unhappy guest receives a note from the hotel manager with the bottle of wine. Complete the note with words from the box.

| smoke | can | Thank you | apologies | room | superior | accept |

Dear Ms Hepworth,

Please (1) _____ my (2) _____ for the smell of (3) _____ in your (4) _____. (5) _____ for bringing it to our attention. I hope that your (6) _____ room is to your satisfaction.

Please accept this bottle of wine with the compliments of the hotel. I hope you enjoy the rest of your stay. If there is anything else I (7) _____ do for you, please don't hesitate to contact me or my staff.

Yours sincerely,

J Heathcote

Jim Heathcote
General Manager

Guest problems | Unit 10

Speaking

5 You are working at Reception when an unhappy guest calls. Read the cues and deal with the problem. Play Track 40 and speak after the beep. You start. Then listen to Track 41 to compare your conversation.

You	(*Answer the internal phone call politely.*)
Guest	Hello. There is a problem with my room!
You	(*Say sorry politely and ask what the problem is.*)
Guest	I've just checked into Room 762 and I'm not happy. My room hasn't been cleaned. The bathroom is still dirty.
You	(*Say sorry again.*)
Guest	Well? What are you going to do about it?
You	(*Tell caller she can have a new room; tell her to wait in the room for Guest Services to collect the guest's bags.*)
Guest	OK. Thanks.

Now you call Guest Services.

Guest Services	Hello, Guest Services. Simon speaking.
You	(*Ask Simon to go to Room 762 to move the guest's bags to Room 1112.*)
Guest Services	OK.
You	(*Say thank you.*)

Now you can
Deal with complaints from guests
Find solutions to problems
Move guests to a new room

Hotel & Hospitality English | 45

11 At breakfast

Saying where things are | Offering food and drink | Taking breakfast orders

Conversations

1 David works in Metro Hotel's restaurant. This morning he is serving breakfast. Listen to his conversations.

A	David	Good morning. **Could I have your room number, please?**
	Guest 1	Morning. We're in Room 406.
	David	Thank you. **The continental breakfast is on the buffet** over there. **Feel free to help yourselves. Here are your menus** if you'd like something from the kitchen. **I'll come and take your orders in a moment. Can I bring you** some tea or coffee?
	Guest 1	Coffee for me, please, with hot milk.
	Guest 2	And tea for me.
	David	What kind of tea would you like?
	Guest 2	English breakfast, please. With milk. And could we have some toast?
	David	Of course. Would you like white, brown or wholemeal?
	Guest 2	Wholemeal, please.

Hotel & Hospitality English

At breakfast | Unit 11

B

David	Here's your tea and coffee, and your toast. **Would you like anything from the menu?**	
Guest 1	I'll have the sausages, scrambled eggs, and hash browns.	
David	Madam?	
Guest 2	I'd like the blueberry pancakes, please.	
David	Thank you. I'll get those for you right away. [...]	
David	**Here you are. Enjoy your breakfasts. Is there anything else I can get you?**	
Guest 2	No, thanks.	

Did you know?

At breakfast there are several ways to cook eggs: soft / hard boiled, scrambled, fried, poached and in an omelette. In the US, there are many different ways to ask for fried eggs to be cooked, for example *over easy*, which means cooked on both sides, and *sunny side up*, which means cooked on one side.

Understanding

2 Listen to the conversations again and complete the order for breakfast.

```
_____ x coffee with milk
1 x _____ with milk
1 x wholemeal _____
1 x sausages, _____ eggs,
and hash _____
1 x blueberry _____
```

Key phrases

Breakfast orders

Could I have your room number, please?	Can I bring you …?
The continental breakfast is on the buffet.	What kind of tea / bread would you like?
(Feel free to) help yourselves / yourself to the buffet.	Would you like anything from the menu?
Here are your menus.	Here you are.
I'll come and take your orders in a moment.	Enjoy (your breakfast).
	Is there anything else I can get you?

Hotel & Hospitality English

Practice

3 Put the words in the sentences into the correct order.

1 free help to Feel yourselves
   _____.

2 please your number room have I Could?
   _____?

3 bring you Can coffee I some
   _____?

4 menu Would anything the you from like
   _____?

5 breakfast Enjoy your
   _____.

4 Complete the sentences in this conversation. Then listen to Track 43 to check your answers.

David Good morning, madam. Could I have your room (1) _____, please?

Guest It's 469.

David Thank you. The continental breakfast is on the (2) _____. Feel free to help (3) _____. Here's the (4) _____ if you'd like to order something from the kitchen.

Guest Thanks. Could I have some coffee?

David Of (5) _____. I'll (6) _____ some right (7) _____.

David Here's your (8) _____. (9) _____ you like anything from the menu?

Guest No, thanks.

David Enjoy your (10) _____.

Hotel & Hospitality English

At breakfast | Unit 11

Speaking

Language tip

Say *Here you are* when you give plates of food to guests. You can also say *Here / There you go*.

Say *right away* to show you will do something quickly. You can also use *straight away* in British English and *coming right up* in American English.

5 You are serving at breakfast. Read the cues and take the guest's breakfast order. Play Track 44 and speak after the beep. You start. Then listen to Track 45 to compare your conversation.

You	(*Say hello to guest politely.*)
Guest	Good morning.
You	(*Ask for room number.*)
Guest	I'm staying in Room 872.
You	(*Continental breakfast or something from the menu?*)
Guest	I haven't decided yet.
You	(*Give guest breakfast menu.*)
Guest	Thank you.
You	(*Ask if she wants tea or coffee.*)
Guest	Could I have a pot of Earl Grey tea, please?
You	(*Milk or lemon?*)
Guest	Lemon, please.
You	(*Offer guest toast.*)
Guest	Yes please. And I don't think I'll have anything from the menu.
You	(*Invite guest to go to buffet.*)
Guest	Thank you.
You	(*Give guest tea and end conversation politely.*)

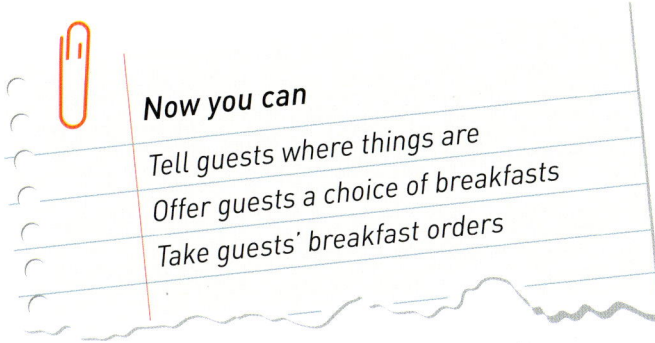

Now you can

Tell guests where things are
Offer guests a choice of breakfasts
Take guests' breakfast orders

Hotel & Hospitality English | 49

12 At the bar

Taking orders at the bar | Recommending something | Taking payment

Conversations

1 David is working in the Metro Hotel's bar. Listen to his conversations.

A

David	Good evening, sir. How are you this evening?
Guest	Fine, thanks.
David	**What can I get you?**
Guest	I'll have a beer, please.
David	Of course, sir. **Would you like draught or bottled beer?**
Guest	I'd like to try a draught beer. What would you recommend?
David	Well, the German and Czech pilsner on draught are very popular.
Guest	Right. I'll have a Czech pilsner, please.
David	There you are, sir. **That'll be £3.90, please.**
Guest	Thank you.

Hotel & Hospitality English

At the bar | Unit 12

B

David	Good evening, ladies. What would you like this evening?
Guest	Two gin and tonics, please – and could we have long drinks with lots of ice please?
David	Of course. **Would you like a slice of lemon?**
Guest	Yes, please.
David	Here you are. **Would you like to pay for them now** or **shall I start a tab for you?**
Guest	I think we'll start a tab. We might have another drink later on.
David	Of course. Could you give me your room number, please?
Guest	I'm in 469.
David	**Could you sign here, please?**
Guest	Thank you.

Did you know?

In American English the phrase *on tap* is a more common way of saying *on draught*.

Understanding

2 Listen to the conversations again and decide if the statements below are True or False.

1 The man chooses a bottled beer. T / F
2 David recommends beers from Germany and the Czech Republic. T / F
3 The ladies don't want ice and lemon in their drinks. T / F
4 The ladies are not staying in the hotel. T / F
5 The ladies want to pay for their drinks later in the evening. T / F

Key phrases

At the bar

What can I get you?	*Would you like to pay for them now?*
Would you like draught or bottled beer?	*Shall I start a tab for you?*
That'll be [price], please.	*Could you sign here, please?*
Would you like ice / a slice of lemon?	

Hotel & Hospitality English | 51

Practice

3 Fill in the missing letters to complete the sentences.

1 W__ t c__ __ I __ __ t you?
2 S__ __ __ ll st__ __ t a t__ __ f__ __ you?
3 W__ __ l__ you __ __ __ e i__ __ and l__ __ on?
4 W__ __ ld you li__ __ b__ __ t__ __ d or __ra__ __ h__ beer?

4 Put this dialogue between David and a hotel guest into the correct order. Then listen to Track 47 to check your answers. The first one has been done for you.

	David:	Would you like ice?
1	David:	Good evening, sir. How are you this evening?
	Guest:	I'm fine, thank you.
	Guest:	Can you charge it to my room?
	Guest:	Scotch and soda, please.
	Guest:	No, thank you.
	Guest:	It's 1107.
	David:	That'll be £6.00, please.
	David:	What can I get you?
	David:	Of course, sir. Can you give me your room number?

At the bar | Unit 12

> **Language tip**
>
> When you say prices, first say the main number, second the currency – although this part is optional –, and third the smaller numbers, for example: *six (euros) ninety* [€6.90], *two (pounds) fifty* [£2.50], *three (dollars) ninety-nine* [$3.99].

Speaking

5 Listen to these prices and repeat them.

1 £9.99   2 €3.20   3 £11.50   4 $147.90   5 €16.45

6 You are working at the bar. Read the cues and take the guest's order. Play Track 49 and speak after the beep. You start.
Then listen to Track 50 to compare your conversation.

You	(Say hello to guest politely.)
Guest	Good evening, how are you?
You	(Answer politely and ask guest what he would like to drink.)
Guest	I think I'll have a beer. What bottled beers do you have?
You	(Tell guest Grolsch, Heineken and Budweiser.)
Guest	What would you recommend?
You	(Choose one of the three beers yourself and recommend it.)
Guest	Fine. Then I'll have one of those.
You	(Give beer to guest.)
Guest	How much do I owe you?
You	(Tell guest £4.00.)
Guest	Can I put it on a tab?
You	(Tell guest yes and ask for his room number.)
Guest	I'm staying in Room 406.
You	(Thank him and ask guest for signature.)

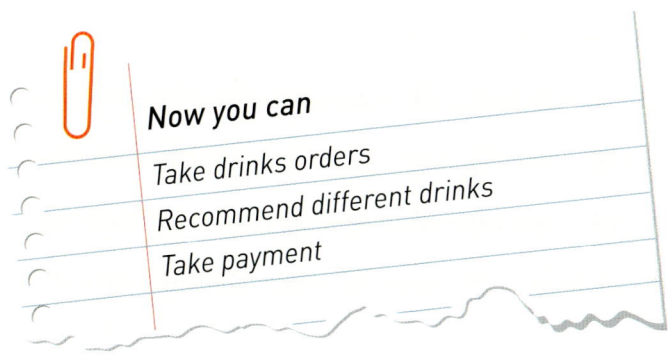

Now you can
- Take drinks orders
- Recommend different drinks
- Take payment

Hotel & Hospitality English | 53

13 Complaints from guests at the bar

Dealing with complaints | Apologizing for mistakes | Explaining the bill

Conversations

1 At the bar David has to deal with some unhappy customers. Listen to his conversations.

A

David	Here's your mineral water with ice and lemon, madam.
Guest	I'm sorry, I can't drink out of that. The glass is dirty and there's lipstick around the edge. Please take it away and bring me another one.
David	**I'm very sorry**, madam. **I'll replace it right away.**
Guest	Thank you.
David	Here you are, madam. **I hope this glass is better for you.**
Guest	Yes, that looks a lot better, thank you.
David	My pleasure.
Guest	Excuse me?
David	**Is there another problem**, madam?
Guest	I asked for still mineral water, not sparkling.
David	Oh, sorry. **I do apologize.** I'll exchange it at once.

Hotel & Hospitality English

Complaints from guests at the bar | Unit 13

B

Guest		Excuse me. Could we have the bill, please?
David		Of course, sir. That'll be £55.19, please.
Guest		£55? That's very expensive!
David		Well, **that's for your food and two drinks**, sir, and there's a 15% service charge which is added to the bill.
Guest		Service charge?
David		Yes, sir. If you look at the menu, it says a service charge of 15% is added to your bill. **I'm afraid it's hotel policy**, sir.

Did you know?

In British English guests ask for the *bill*. In American English they ask for the *check*.

Understanding

2 Listen to the conversations again and answer the following questions.

1 In conversation A, what drink has the guest ordered from the bar?
2 What is the problem with her glass?
3 Why is she unhappy with her drink?
4 Why is the guest in conversation B not satisfied?
5 How much is the service charge?

Key phrases

Dealing with complaints at the bar

I'm very / really sorry.	I do apologize.
I'll replace it right away.	That's for your food and two drinks.
I hope this one is better for you.	I'm afraid it's hotel policy.
Is there a / another problem?	

Hotel & Hospitality English | 55

Practice

3 Put the words in the sentences into the correct order.

1 away back I'll bar the take right to it
   _____ .

2 afraid hotel policy I'm it's
   _____ .

3 better one hope for I you is this
   _____ .

4 madam Is a problem, there
   _____ ?

4 Choose the right word to complete these sentences.

1 Here's your mineral water _____ ice and lemon.
   by   of   with
2 I'll take it back _____ the bar.
   from   to   at
3 Look _____ the menu.
   at   by   to
4 The service charge is added _____ the bill.
   with   to   by
5 The glass has lipstick _____ it.
   on   by   of

Language tip

Stress the second syllable in numbers 13, 14, 15, 16, 17, 18 and 19 like this *fifteen* so they do not sound like 30, 40, 50 and so on.

Language tip

Add *do* to make *I apologize* sound stronger, for example *I **do** apologize*.

With *I'm sorry*, stress *am* to make it sound stronger, for example *I **am** sorry*.

Complaints from guests at the bar | Unit 13

Speaking

5 Practise making stronger apologies. Listen to Track 02 to compare your answers.

1 I'm sorry that your food is cold, madam.
 You: _____.

2 I apologize for the wait, sir.
 You: _____.

3 Sorry that you don't like your table.
 You: _____.

4 I apologize for keeping you waiting.
 You: _____.

6 You are working at the bar. Read the cues and respond to the guest's complaint. Play Track 03 and speak after the beep. You start. Then listen to Track 04 to compare your conversation.

Guest   Excuse me, waiter.
You   (Reply politely.)
Guest   There's a problem with my drink.
You   (Ask what the problem is.)
Guest   I asked for still water, not sparkling.
You   (Apologize very politely and tell guest you will change it.)
Guest   Thank you. Please be quick! I'm in a hurry.
You   (Tell guest you'll bring it immediately.)
Guest   Thank you.
You   (Give guest the still water and apologize again.)
Guest   Thanks. That was quick.
You   (Say sorry again and finish conversation politely.)

Now you can

Deal with complaints from guests
Apologize for wrong food / drink orders
Explain charges on the bill

Hotel & Hospitality English

14 In the restaurant (1)

Welcoming diners | Giving out menus | Taking drinks orders

Conversation

1 Danielle is welcoming diners to the restaurant. Listen to her conversation.

A

Danielle	Good evening sir, madam. **Welcome to the Metro restaurant. May I take your coats?**
Diner 1	Good evening. Thanks.
Danielle	**Would you like an aperitif before you order?**
Diner 2	Yes, please. Could we have two glasses of prosecco?
Danielle	Certainly. **Let me give you some menus. I'll come back to take your order in a few moments.**
Diner 1	That's wonderful, thank you.
Danielle	Of course. We also have some specials on the board.
Diner 2	What are the specials?
Danielle	**The specials today are** rack of lamb, lemon sole and a vegetarian pasta dish.

Hotel & Hospitality English

In the restaurant (1) | Unit 14

Later

B	Danielle	Here you are. Two glasses of prosecco. **Are you having wine this evening?**
	Diner 1	Thank you. Yes, we are.
	Danielle	**Here's the wine list.** We have four excellent red and white house wines and on the last pages you'll find the full wine list.
	Diner 1	Thank you.
	Danielle	**Let me know when you're ready to order.**

Did you know?

Prosecco is an Italian sparkling wine.

Understanding

2   Listen to the conversation again and answer these questions.

1   What two things does Danielle offer to do when the diners arrive?
2   What do the diners order as an aperitif?
3   Does Danielle take their order immediately?
4   Name two dishes that are on the specials board.
5   How many house wines are on the wine list?

Key phrases

In the restaurant

Welcome to the (Metro) restaurant.	The specials today are … .
May I take your coat?	Are you having wine this evening?
Would you like an aperitif before you order?	Here's the wine list.
Let me give you some menus.	Let me know when you're ready to order.
I'll come back to take your order in a few moments.	

Hotel & Hospitality English

Practice

3 Put the words in the sentences into the correct order.

1 take coats your I May
   _____ ?

2 you Can aperitif bring I an
   _____ ?

3 menus give me Let some you
   _____ .

4 order me to know are you when Let ready
   _____ .

5 the list wine Would see like to you
   _____ ?

6 a moments come few in your back I'll order take to.
   _____ .

4 This waiter is very impolite. Rephrase what he says to make the sentences more polite.

1 Give me your coat!
2 Hi. Thanks for coming to eat here!
3 Here. Take the menu!
4 You want wine?
5 Tell me when you've decided what you want to eat.

5 A lot of French words are used in restaurants. Can you match these French restaurant terms to their explanation?

French word or phrase		Explanation
1	*digestif*	A The person in charge of a restaurant who welcomes diners and gives orders to the waiters
2	*aperitif*	B A style of menu in a restaurant where each dish has a separate price
3	*maitre d'*	C A meal served in a restaurant at a fixed price, with a limited number of dishes to choose from
4	*à la carte*	D An alcoholic drink that people drink before a meal
5	*table d'hôte*	E An alcoholic drink that people drink after a meal

Hotel & Hospitality English

In the restaurant (1) | Unit 14

Speaking

> **Language tip**
>
> Use *May I* as in *May I take your coat?* to sound especially polite in a formal situation like welcoming diners to a restaurant.

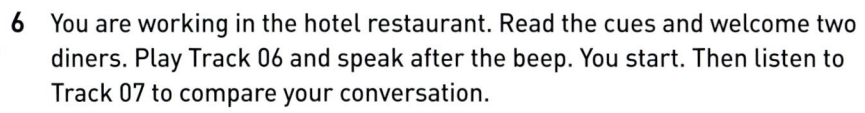

6. You are working in the hotel restaurant. Read the cues and welcome two diners. Play Track 06 and speak after the beep. You start. Then listen to Track 07 to compare your conversation.

You	(*Say good evening politely and welcome diners.*)
Diner 1	Thank you. We have a table reserved for 8 pm in the name of Johansson.
You	(*Reply politely and offer to take their coats.*)
Diner 2	Thank you. That's very kind.
You	(*Ask if they want an aperitif.*)
Diner 1	Yes, please. I'll have a gin and tonic.
Diner 2	And I'd like a Campari and soda.
You	(*Give them the menus and tell them you will bring their drinks right away.*)
Diner 2	Thank you.
You	(*Ask diners if they want the wine list.*)
Diner 1	Yes, please.
You	(*Give diners the wine list.*)
Diner 2	The food all looks delicious. I'm very hungry. Are there any specials this evening?
You	(*Tell diner that they are on the specials board behind her.*)
Diner 2	OK. I'll take a look.
You	(*Tell diners you will return soon to take their order.*)

Now you can

Welcome diners to the restaurant
Give diners the menu and wine list
Serve their drinks

Hotel & Hospitality English

15 In the restaurant (2)

Taking food orders | Explaining dishes | Choosing drinks

Conversations

1 Danielle is very busy in the restaurant. Listen to her conversation with one table.

Danielle	Good evening, everyone. **Are you ready to order?**
Diner 1	Not quite. I think we need a little bit longer. Please tell us the specials again.
Danielle	Of course, madam. On the specials board this evening we have lemon sole, rack of lamb and a vegetarian pasta dish.
Diner 2	It all sounds so nice. I don't know what to have!
Danielle	**Take your time.** I'll be back in a few minutes to take your orders.

Later

Diner 1	Excuse me, I think we're ready to order now.
Danielle	Very good, madam. **What are you going to have?**
Diner 1	No appetizers to start. I'll have the lemon sole and can we have one steak, cooked medium rare, please?

Hotel & Hospitality English

In the restaurant (2) | Unit 15

Danielle	Excellent choices. **And have you chosen some wine?**
Diner 2	Yes, we'll have a bottle of the house red, please.
Danielle	Of course, sir. Would you like some water too?
Diner 2	Yes, a bottle of still, and one sparkling.

Did you know?

In British English the three parts of a meal are the *starter* or *appetizer*, *main course* and *dessert*, *sweet* or *pudding*. In American English they are *appetizer*, *main course* or *entrée*, and *dessert*.

Understanding

2 Listen to the conversation again and take the order.

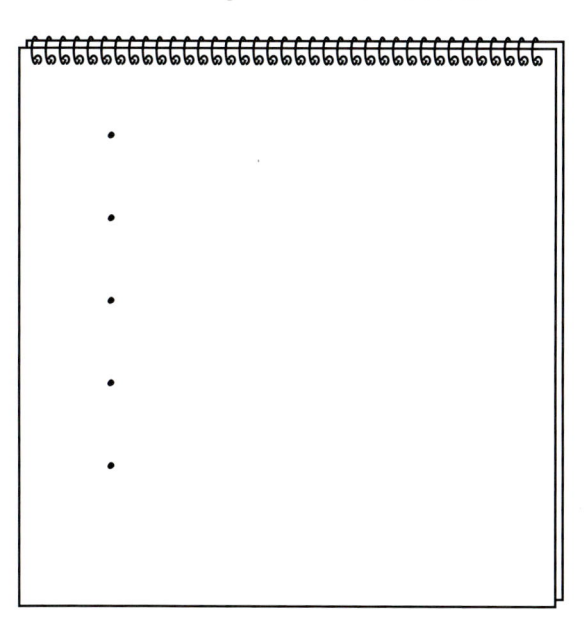

-
-
-
-
-

Key phrases

In the restaurant	
Are you ready to order?	*What are you going to have?*
Take your time.	*Have you chosen some wine?*

Hotel & Hospitality English

Practice

3 Put the sentences into the correct order. The first one has been done for you. Listen to Track 09 to check your answer.

1	Danielle:	Good afternoon, madam. Are you ready to order?
	Danielle:	Very good, madam. What are you going to have?
	Danielle:	Of course. Still or sparkling?
	Diner:	Not quite. Please give me five more minutes.
	Diner:	I'll have pâté as an appetizer and then a Caesar salad with chicken, please.
	Danielle:	Of course. I'll be back in a moment.
	Diner:	No, thank you. But could I have a bottle of water?
	Danielle:	Excuse me, I'm ready to order now.
	Danielle:	An excellent choice, madam. Are you going to have a glass of wine?
	Diner:	Still please, with ice and lemon.

Speaking

4 Practise using *going to* to ask diners questions. Listen to Track 10 to compare your answers.

1 you / order / some wine, sir?
You: _____?
2 you / have / an appetizer, madam?
You: _____?
3 you / have / a dessert?
You: _____?
4 What / you / have for your main course?
You: _____?

Hotel & Hospitality English

In the restaurant (2) | Unit 15

5 You are serving two diners in the restaurant. Read the cues given and take their orders. Play Track 11 and speak after the beep. You start. Then listen to Track 12 to compare your conversation.

You	(*Ask diners if they are ready to order.*)
Diner 1	Yes, we are. Thank you.
You	(*Ask the woman what she wants to eat.*)
Diner 1	I'll start with the soup, please, and I'd like the mixed grill for my main course.
You	(*Ask the man what he wants to eat.*)
Diner 2	I'd like oysters as an appetizer, please, and a seafood salad for my main course.
You	(*Ask if they are having wine.*)
Diner 1	Yes, please. A small glass of Shiraz.
Diner 2	And a large glass of Sauvignon Blanc.
You	(*Ask if they want water.*)
Diner 1	Yes, please. A bottle of Perrier.
You	(*Say politely that you don't serve Perrier.*)
Diner 1	Oh, I see. What kinds of sparkling water do you have?
You	(*Tell diners: San Pellegrino, Voss or Poland Spring.*)
Diner 1	Then we'll have a bottle of Poland Spring, please.
You	(*Praise the choice, finish conversation politely by saying you'll bring drinks quickly.*)

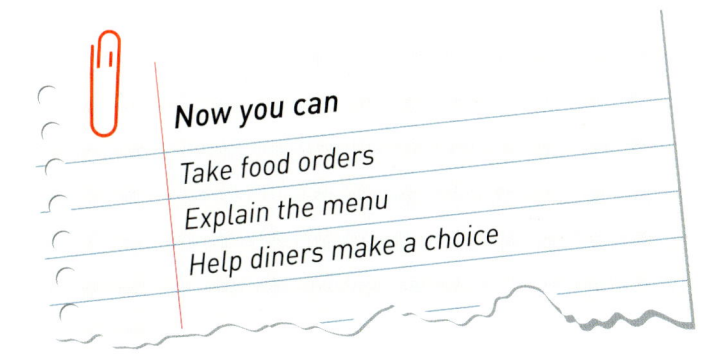

Now you can

Take food orders
Explain the menu
Help diners make a choice

Hotel & Hospitality English

16 In the restaurant (3)

Asking about dessert and coffee | Bringing the bill | Handling payment

Conversation

1 Danielle is attending to two diners who have finished their main courses. Listen to her conversation.

Danielle	Sorry to interrupt. **May I clear away your plates?**	
Diner 1	Yes, please do. We've finished.	
Danielle	**How were your main courses? Was everything OK?**	
Diner 2	Yes, thank you. It was all excellent.	
Danielle	**Would you like to see the dessert menu?**	
Diner 2	No, thank you. I think we'll skip dessert.	
Danielle	**Can I bring you anything else?** A coffee or a *digestif*, perhaps?	
Diner 2	Could we just have two espressos?	
Danielle	Of course.	
Diner 1	And then could I have the bill, please?	
Danielle	Of course, sir. I'll be back right away with your coffees.	
Diner 1	Can I pay by credit card?	

Hotel & Hospitality English

In the restaurant (3) | Unit 16

Danielle	Yes, sir. ... **Oh, I'm afraid we don't accept that kind of credit card**, sir, only VISA and MasterCard.
Diner 1	OK. Then I'll use my VISA card.
Danielle	Here's your bill, sir. **Please put your card in the terminal, enter your PIN, and then press the green OK button.**

Did you know?

In the UK an optional service charge of between 10% and 15% is often added to a restaurant bill. This can also be called a discretionary service charge. This means that diners don't need to leave a tip in addition to that. In the US, a service charge of between 15% and 17% is also often added to the bill of larger parties. Otherwise, diners are expected to leave a tip of at least 15%.

Understanding

2 Listen to the conversation again and answer the following questions.

1. Are the diners going to have dessert?
2. Do the diners order anything else?
3. How does the diner want to pay?
4. Which credit cards does the restaurant accept?
5. What is the problem with the diner's first credit card?
6. List the three instructions that Danielle gives to the diner.

Key phrases

Finishing the meal

May I clear away your plates?	*Can I bring you anything else?*
How were your main courses / was your meal?	*We accept … . I'm afraid we don't accept … .*
Was everything OK?	*Put your card in the terminal. Enter your PIN number. Press the green OK button.*
Would you like to see the dessert menu?	

Hotel & Hospitality English

Practice

3 Use the words in the box to complete the conversation.

| afraid | use | enter | press | by | Was | accept | May |

Danielle (1) _____ I clear away the plates?
Diner Of course.
Danielle (2) _____ everything OK?
Diner Yes, fine, thanks. Can I pay the bill (3) _____ credit card?
Danielle Yes, but I'm (4) _____ we don't (5) _____ that kind of credit card, madam.
Diner OK. Then I'll (6) _____ my VISA card.
Danielle Here's your bill, madam. Please put your card in the terminal, (7) _____ your PIN, and then (8) _____ the green OK button.

Did you know?

A card like VISA or MasterCard is a **credit card**. The other form of payment card that users can use to pay for goods and withdraw money from a cash machine is called a **debit card**.

Chip and Pin is not widely used in the US yet, and can cause problems for Americans when they travel abroad.

Language tip

When you ask *A coffee or digestif, perhaps?* make sure it sounds like a real question by raising the pitch of your voice at the end of the statement.

Speaking

4 Listen to these questions and repeat them.

1. Was everything OK?
2. Do you want coffee or tea?
3. Would you like to pay by credit card?
4. A coffee or a *digestif*, perhaps?
5. Rare or medium rare?

In the restaurant (3) | Unit 16

5 A couple in the restaurant have finished their main courses. Read the cues and attend to the diners. Play Track 15 and speak after the beep. You start. Then listen to Track 16 to compare your conversation.

You	(Ask diners if they have finished their meal.)
Diner 1	Yes we have, thank you.
You	(Ask if they enjoyed their meal.)
Diner 2	Yes, it was very good. My steak was perfectly cooked.
You	(Reply politely. Ask if they want dessert.)
Diner 1	No, thank you. I don't think we could eat anything else.
You	(Coffee?)
Diner 2	Yes, please. Two espressos.
You	(Ask if they want anything else.)
Diner 1	No, thanks. Could I have our bill, please?
You	(Say you'll bring the espressos and the bill immediately.)
Diner 1	Do you accept traveller's cheques?
You	(Tell diner politely that you don't accept traveller's cheques, only cash or credit cards.)
Diner 1	OK. Do you take AMEX?
You	(Tell diner Yes.)
Diner 2	Is service included?
You	(Tell diner a 15% service charge has been added to the bill; give payment terminal to diner and explain what to do.)
Diner 1	Done. There you are.
You	(Thank diner.)

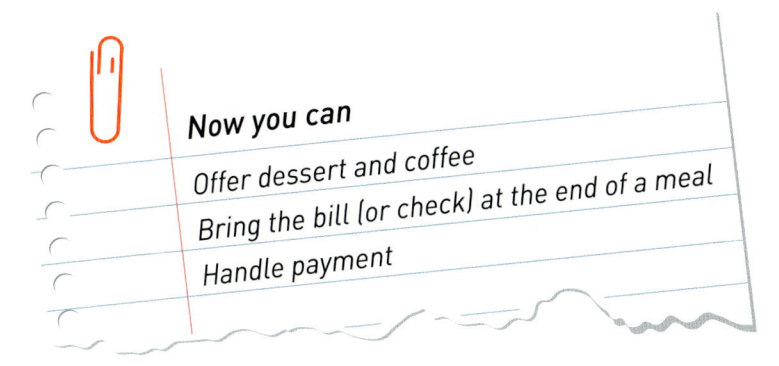

Now you can
Offer dessert and coffee
Bring the bill (or check) at the end of a meal
Handle payment

Hotel & Hospitality English | 69

17 Housekeeping

Briefing new staff | Explaining hotel rules | Answering questions

Conversation

1 Karen, a senior housekeeper, is briefing a new maid. Listen to the conversation.

Karen	**Make sure that you** replace the hot drinks packets every day: enough for four cups a day – two per person.
Maid	Where can I find the supplies?
Karen	There's a supplies cabinet on every floor. The toiletries, soap and toilet paper are also stored there. **Every room must have** three rolls of toilet paper at all times.
Maid	Do I have to change the sheets every day?
Karen	No, **you don't have to**. Only do it if the guest asks you to. But, if a guest is staying for more than three nights, **you must** change the sheets on the fourth day.
Maid	What about the pillowcases?
Karen	**Change them every day.** They're in the linen cabinet with the towels and bathrobes.
Maid	Do I have to vacuum under the bed every day?

Hotel & Hospitality English

Karen	Yes. Also, dust and polish all the surfaces, and **pay special attention to** the mirrors and TV screen. But **you mustn't clean** the TV screen with water.
Maid	OK.
Karen	And **don't forget to** replace the TV remote control in the holder!

Did you know?

In British English it is *toilet*, *ladies* or *gents*. In American English it is *restroom*, *bathroom*, or *washroom*. In American English *toilet* is impolite.

Understanding

2 Listen to the conversation again and answer these questions.
1. How many hot drinks packets must there be in the room every day?
2. Where are hot drinks packets and supplies stored?
3. How many toilet rolls must there be in the bathroom at all times?
4. Does the maid have to change the sheets every day?
5. Does the maid have to change the pillowcases every day?

Key phrases

Giving instructions to a maid

Make sure that you	*Change the ... every day*
Every room must have	*Pay special attention to ... .*
You have to / don't have to	*You mustn't ... .*
You must	*Don't forget to ... .*

Practice

3 Identify these bedroom and bathroom objects. Use the words in the box.

> towels bathrobe toilet roll toiletries soap
> bed drinks packets cups safe

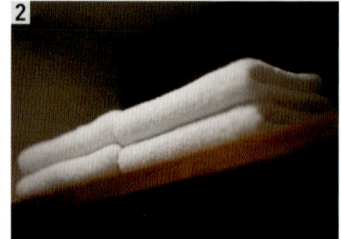

4 Choose the correct option in these sentences.
1 Make sure that you **clean / cleaning** under the bed.
2 Don't forget **dusting / to dust** the mirror in the bedroom.
3 You must **change / to change** the pillowcases every day.
4 You **don't have / don't have to** change the sheets every day.
5 Dust and **polish / polishing** all the surfaces.

Language tip

Use *must* or *have to* to say something is necessary, for example, *You must / have to clean the room every day.*

Use *don't have to* to say something is not necessary, for example, *You don't have to change the sheets every day.*

Use *must not* or *mustn't* to tell someone not to do something.
You mustn't / must not clean the TV screen with water.

Use *Do I have to ... ?* in questions.

Hotel & Hospitality English

Housekeeping | Unit 17

Speaking

5 Practise using *must, mustn't, have to* and *don't have to*. Make sentences starting with *You*. Listen to Track 18 to compare your answers.

1 have to – polish – TV [necessary]
   _____.

2 have to – clean – windows [not necessary]
   _____.

3 must – replace – drinks packets [necessary]
   _____.

4 mustn't – clean – TV screen with water [not allowed]
   _____.

6 You are giving instructions to a new maid who has lots of questions. Read the cues and give her instructions. Play Track 19 and speak after the beep. The new maid starts. Then listen to Track 20 to compare your answers.

Maid	How often do I have to vacuum the room?
You	(*Every day.*)
Maid	Even under the bed?
You	(*Say yes, it is necessary.*)
Maid	When do I change the sheets?
You	(*Only on fourth morning.*)
Maid	And do I change the pillowcases every fourth day too?
You	(*No: every day.*)
Maid	How many coffee and tea packets do I put in the room?
You	(*Two per person per day.*)
Maid	Should I clean the TV screen with water?
You	(*No, say you mustn't. Just use a duster.*)

Now you can

Give instructions to new staff
Explain hotel rules to a new maid
Answer staff questions

Hotel & Hospitality English | 73

18 Housekeeping problems

Dealing with requests | Solving problems | Agreeing to come back later

Conversations

1 Karen Dawson has to deal with some housekeeping problems. Listen to her conversations.

A

Karen	Good morning, Housekeeping. Karen speaking.
Guest	Hello. Can you bring us some extra pillows, please?
Karen	Of course, sir. **How many would you like?**
Guest	Could we have four extra ones, please?
Karen	Certainly, sir. **What's your room number?**
Guest	It's Room 406.
Karen	**I'll send them up as soon as I can**, sir.

Hotel & Hospitality English

Housekeeping problems | Unit 18

B
Karen		Good morning, Housekeeping. Karen speaking.
Guest		Is that Housekeeping?
Karen		Yes, it is. How can I help you?
Guest		We've just come back to Room 369 and our room hasn't been cleaned. The breakfast dishes haven't been taken away and the bed hasn't been made. And we need some fresh towels.
Karen		Oh, I'm very sorry, madam. I'll send a maid up right away to clean the room.

C
Karen		Housekeeping. **Sorry to disturb you. I've come to clean your room.**
Guest		Could you come back later, please? We're not ready.
Karen		Of course. Sorry about that. **Please hang the 'Please Tidy My Room' sign on the door when you're ready.**
Guest		OK. Thank you.

Understanding

2 Listen to the conversations again and answer the following questions.

1 In which conversation does the guest have a complaint, A, B or C?
2 In which conversation does the guest want something brought to the room, A, B or C?
3 Name two reasons why the guest in conversation B isn't happy.
4 Why won't the guest in conversation C let Karen enter the room?
5 What does Karen ask the guest in conversation C to do?

Key phrases

Housekeeping problems

How many [extra ...] would you like?	*I've come to clean your room.*
What's your room number?	*Please hang the sign on the door when you're ready.*
I'll send it / them up as soon as I can.	
Sorry to disturb you.	

Hotel & Hospitality English

Practice

3 Match the two halves to make sentences.

1 I've come
2 I'll
3 I'm sorry
4 I'll come
5 How many
6 How can

A send somebody up immediately.
B to clean your room.
C I help you?
D to disturb you.
E back when you've finished.
F do you need?

> **Language tip**
>
> Use *bring* when you want someone to move something toward a person [here], for example, *I'll bring the towels to your room*. [The guest is in this room.]
>
> Use *take* when you want someone to move something to another location [there], for example, *Maria, take the towels to Room 124*. [Maria is not in Room 124.]

4 Complete the sentences using *bring* or *take*.

1 Ali, can you _____ this new bathrobe to Room 1015?
2 Our pillows are too soft. Could you _____ us some firmer ones, please?
3 Where are you going? – Karen asked me to _____ these pillows to Room 254.
4 Hello, Mr Norman. This is Karen from Housekeeping. One of the maids will _____ the new pillows to your room immediately.

> **Language tip**
>
> Use *Certainly* or *Of course* to respond to requests by guests and to say that you will do something.

Hotel & Hospitality English

Housekeeping problems | Unit 18

Speaking

5 You are on duty in Housekeeping when the phone rings. Read the cues given and deal with the guest's problem. Play Track 22 and speak after the beep. You start. Then listen to Track 23 to compare your conversation.

You	*(Answer by saying your name and department and asking what the caller wants.)*
Guest	Good morning. We have a problem with our bed. Can you help?
You	*(Answer positively and ask what problem is.)*
Guest	My husband says the pillows are too soft. He says they hurt his neck.
You	*(Offer to bring different / extra pillows – ask how many.)*
Guest	That would be great. Could you bring six?
You	*(Agree and ask for room number.)*
Guest	We're on the tenth floor in Suite 1023.
You	*(Tell guest you will do it immediately.)*
Guest	Thank you very much.
You	*(Reply to guest's thanks and end call politely.)*

6 You are moving from room to room to clean them. Read the cues given. Play Track 24 and speak after the beep. You start. Then listen to Track 25 to compare your conversation.

(Knock on the door)

You	*(Say who you are and what you want.)*
Guest	Please don't come in. We're still in bed.
You	*(Say sorry and tell guest you'll come back later.)*
Guest	Thank you.
You	*(Ask guest to use sign to let you know when he wants room cleaned.)*

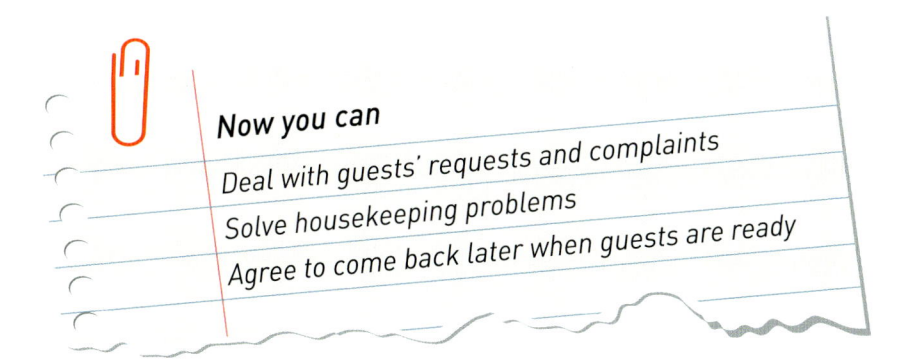

Now you can

Deal with guests' requests and complaints
Solve housekeeping problems
Agree to come back later when guests are ready

Hotel & Hospitality English

19 Room service

Taking room service orders | Agreeing delivery times | Delivering room service

Conversations

1 David is also responsible for room service orders. Listen to his conversations.

26 CD2

A

David	Room Service, can I help you?	
Guest	Good morning. Can I order some room service?	
David	Of course, madam. **What would you like?**	
Guest	I'd like a continental breakfast.	
David	Very good, madam. **Would you like tea or coffee?**	
Guest	Coffee. Could I have a cappuccino?	
David	Certainly, madam.	
Guest	How long will that be? I'm in a hurry this morning.	
David	**It'll be with you in ten minutes.**	
Guest	Good.	
David	**Could I have your room number, please?**	
Guest	It's 1002. Mrs Hepworth.	
David	Thank you, Mrs Hepworth. Goodbye.	
Guest	Thank you. Goodbye.	

Hotel & Hospitality English

B

Guest	One moment. Just coming!	
David	Good morning, madam. Room Service.	
Guest	That was quick.	
David	One continental breakfast with a cappuccino. **Could you sign here please, madam?** Thank you. **Enjoy your breakfast.**	
Guest	Thanks.	

Did you know?

Cappuccino is an Italian way of serving coffee. Traditionally in Italy it is only served in the morning.

A continental breakfast usually includes coffee or tea, a *croissant* with butter and jam or preserve, and fresh fruit.

Understanding

2 Listen to the conversations again and answer the following questions.

1. What kind of breakfast does the guest order?
2. What kind of coffee does the guest order?
3. How quickly will the guest get her breakfast?
4. Why does the guest want her breakfast quickly?

Key phrases

Room Service

What would you like?	*Could I have your room number, please?*
Would you like tea or coffee?	*Could you sign here, please?*
It'll be with you in (about) ... minutes.	*Enjoy your breakfast.*

Hotel & Hospitality English

Practice

3 Put this conversation in the correct order. The first and last lines have already been done for you.

	David:	Very good, madam. Would you like tea or coffee?
1	David:	Room Service, can I help you?
	David:	Of course, madam. What would you like?
13	David:	Thank you.
	Guest:	Good morning. Can I order breakfast?
	Guest:	I'd like a boiled egg with wholemeal toast and fresh fruit.
	Guest:	How long will that be? I have a meeting in an hour.
	Guest:	Tea, please. English breakfast with milk.
	David:	Certainly, madam.
	Guest:	Good.
	David:	Could I have your room number?
	Guest:	It's 745.
	David:	It'll be with you in 15 minutes.

Room service | Unit 19

Speaking

4 You have to take and deliver the room service orders. Read the cues given and take the guest's order. Play Track 27 and speak after the beep. You start. Then listen to Track 28 to compare your conversation.

> **You** (*Answer phone by saying department and your name and asking what the caller wants.*)
> **Guest** Good evening. Is it too late to order some room service?
> **You** (*Tell guest it's not too late and ask what guest wants.*)
> **Guest** Could I have a Metroburger with fries and a beer?
> **You** (*Reply politely and ask guest what kind of beer.*)
> **Guest** I'll have a Budweiser, please.
> **You** (*Ask guest if he wants ketchup with his burger.*)
> **Guest** Yes, please. How long will that be?
> **You** (*Tell guest about 15 minutes and end call politely.*)

5 You are delivering a room service order. You have just knocked on the guest's door. Read the cues given and deliver the order. Play Track 29 and speak after the beep. You start. Then listen to Track 30 to compare your conversation.

> **Guest** Yes. What is it?
> **You** (*Tell guest who you are and why you are knocking.*)
> **Guest** Oh, right. One moment, please.
> **You** (*Confirm to the guest what you have brought.*)
> **Guest** Just put it down on the table, please.
> **You** (*Do as guest asks and ask guest for a signature.*)
> **Guest** Sure. Here you are.
> **You** (*Thank guest, end conversation politely and say good night.*)

Now you can
Take room service orders
Agree when you will deliver the order
Deliver room service orders

20 Guest services

Ordering things for guests | Making appointments | Checking information

Conversations

1 Simon works in Guest Services. Listen to his conversations.

A

Simon	Good morning, sir. **What can I do for you?**
Guest	Hello. I'd like to order some flowers. It's my wife's birthday tomorrow.
Simon	Of course, sir. What kind of flowers would you like?
Guest	A bouquet of red roses, please. Could you have them delivered tomorrow morning at 9.30?
Simon	Certainly, sir. **I'll take care of that for you.**

B

Simon	Hello, madam. **How can I help you?**
Guest	Is there a hairdresser in the hotel?
Simon	I'm afraid not, madam. But **I can make you an appointment** at a local salon **if you like**.
Guest	Yes, please. Could you do that for me? I'd like an appointment at 11.30. Mrs Lee.
Simon	Of course, Mrs Lee. **I'll call them now.**

Hotel & Hospitality English

C

Guest	Hi, would you look something up for me?
Simon	Yes certainly, madam. **What would you like me to look up for you?**
Guest	Could you check which terminal my flight leaves from? The flight number is EM693 to Dubai.
Simon	One moment. **I'll just check for you.** It leaves from Terminal 3, at 13.50.
Guest	Thanks very much.

Understanding

2 Listen to the conversations again and decide whether the statements are True or False.

1 In conversation A, the guest orders flowers for his wife for their wedding anniversary. T / F
2 There isn't a hairdresser in the hotel. T / F
3 Mrs Lee wants a hair appointment at 11.30. T / F
4 In conversation C, the guest is flying at 15.30. T / F
5 In conversation C, the guest is flying to Dubai. T / F

Key phrases

Guest Services

What can I do for you?	*I'll call them now.*
I'll take care of that for you.	*Would you like me to look something up for you?*
How can I help you?	
I can make you an appointment if you like.	*I'll just check for you.*

Language tip

Use *look up something* (or *look something up*) when you check information on the Internet, for example, *I'll look up the flight times for you.*

Practice

3 Put the words in the sentences into the correct order.

1 you for I'll check just
_____ .

2 something like you for look me up you to Would
_____ ?

3 that care of you for take I'll
_____ .

4 like I can an appointment you if make you
_____ .

4 Complete the sentences with *for*, *of*, *up*, *at*, *on* or *in*.

1 Can you look something _____ for me?
2 I'll check the flight time _____ the Internet.
3 The flight leaves _____ 7.30.
4 What can I do _____ you?
5 The swimming pool opens _____ June.
6 I'll take care _____ that for you.

Language tip

Use *at* in front of times, for example, *at 9.30*. Use *on* in front of days, for example, *on Monday*. Use *in* in front of months, for example, *in September*. In American English say *on the weekend*. In British English say *at the weekend*.

Hotel & Hospitality English

Guest services | Unit 20

Speaking

5 You are working at the Guest Services counter. A guest wants some information. Read the cues and help the woman. Play Track 32 and speak after the beep. You start. Then listen to Track 33 to compare your conversation.

> **You** (*Say hello to guest politely and ask what he wants.*)
> **Guest** Hello. Is there a sauna in the hotel?
> **You** (*Tell the guest yes there is a sauna.*)
> **Guest** Is it open at the weekend?
> **You** (*Tell guest yes.*)
> **Guest** What time does it open today?
> **You** (*Sauna opens: 10 am; closes: 8 pm.*)
> **Guest** Is it a mixed sauna?
> **You** (*Tell guest yes but ladies only: Saturday afternoon.*)
> **Guest** Thank you.
> **You** (*Respond to guest's thanks and end conversation politely.*)

6 You are working at the Guest Services desk. A guest wants some information. Read the cues and help the woman. Play Track 34 and speak after the beep. Then listen to Track 35 to compare your conversation.

> **Guest** Can you look up something on the Internet for me?
> **You** (*Tell guest yes and ask what she wants.*)
> **Guest** Can you check which terminal the Delta flight from Toronto arrives at?
> **You** (*Tell guest you will do it.*)
> **Guest** Thanks.
> **You** (*Tell guest: Delta from Toronto: Terminal 5, 20.15.*)
> **Guest** Thanks.
> **You** (*Respond to guest's thanks and end conversation politely.*)

Now you can

Order things for guests

Offer to make appointments for them

Check information for guests

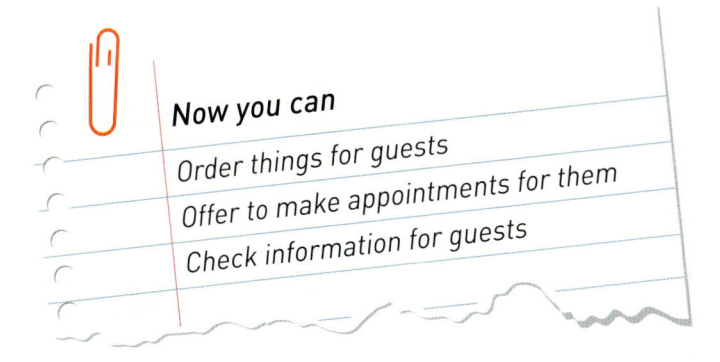

21 In the business centre

Explaining available services | Providing equipment | Providing information

Conversations

🔊 **1** Sarah at the front desk and Simon in the business centre are talking to
36 guests about their IT requirements. Listen to their conversations.
CD2

A | Guest | Hello. My flight's been delayed until this evening. Is there somewhere I could work for a couple of hours?
| Sarah | Yes, of course, madam. **Our business centre has free Wi-Fi for guests** and is very quiet.
| Guest | Thank you. And where is the business centre?
| Sarah | Take the lift up to the second floor and you'll see the entrance in front of you.

B | Guest | Hi, I need to use the Internet but my laptop isn't working.
| Simon | Are you staying here, sir?
| Guest | Yes.
| Simon | Then **you can use the business centre facilities free of charge.**
| Guest | Great. Will I need a password for the computer?
| Simon | Yes, you will and it's printed on this card. **Enter your username MetroRes and this password:** … .

86 | Hotel & Hospitality English

In the business centre | Unit 21

C	Guest	Can I borrow an adaptor, please? The plug on my lead doesn't fit in this socket.
	Simon	Of course, madam. **I can lend you a travel adaptor.** That should fit.
	Guest	Is there a printer here, too? I need to print something out.
	Simon	Yes, madam. **Printouts cost 10 pence per page.**
	Guest	And is it a colour printer?
	Simon	Yes, it is.

Did you know?

In British English you plug your electronic equipment into a *socket*. In American English it is an *outlet*.

Understanding

2 Listen to the conversations again and answer these questions.

1 On which floor is the business centre?
2 Does the guest have to pay to use the business centre?
3 Why does the guest need an adaptor?
4 How much does it cost to print one page?
5 Can the guest print in colour?

Key phrases

Using the business centre

Our business centre has free Internet access / Wi-Fi for guests.	Enter your username […] and this password: … .
You can use the business centre facilities free of charge.	I can lend you a travel adaptor.
	Printouts cost 10 pence per page.

Hotel & Hospitality English

Did you know?

British English spells words like *centre* and *theatre* with *re* at the end. American English spells these words *center* and *theater*. American English omits the letter *u* in words like *color* and *honor*.

Practice

3 Complete these sentences with words from the box.

| on | of | per | up | out | for |

1 I need to print something _____ .
2 Our business centre has free Internet access _____ guests.
3 You can use the business centre facilities free _____ charge.
4 Colour printouts cost 10 pence _____ page.
5 The business centre is _____ the second floor.
6 Take the lift _____ to the second floor.

In the business centre | Unit 21

Speaking

> **Language tip**
>
> Use *borrow* like this: *Can I borrow your pen?*
>
> Use *lend* like this: *Can you lend me your pen? / I can lend you a pen.*

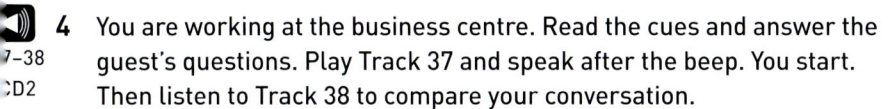

4 You are working at the business centre. Read the cues and answer the guest's questions. Play Track 37 and speak after the beep. You start. Then listen to Track 38 to compare your conversation.

You	(*Say hello to guest politely.*)
Guest	Hi. Is this the business centre? I need to check my emails.
You	(*Answer politely that it is and ask if guest is staying at the hotel.*)
Guest	Yes. I'm in Room 478.
You	(*Explain that business centre is free for guests.*)
Guest	Where can I plug in my laptop?
You	(*Answer and direct guest to a work station.*)
Guest	Oh! My lead doesn't fit in this socket.
You	(*Politely offer to lend guest an adaptor.*)
Guest	That would be great. Thanks a lot.
You	(*Reply to guest's thanks.*)
Guest	Can I use the printer here too?
You	(*Tell guest yes but there is a charge.*)
Guest	How much does it cost?
You	(*Tell guest 10 pence per sheet.*)
Guest	Can I charge it to my room?
You	(*Tell guest yes he can.*)

Now you can

Explain the services that are available for guests to use

Provide equipment for guests

Provide information about the hotel services

Hotel & Hospitality English

22 Recommendations for places to eat

Making restaurant recommendations | Comparing things

Conversations

1 Guests often ask Simon about places to eat locally. Listen to his conversations.

A

Guest 1	Good evening, Simon.	
Simon	Good evening, Mr & Mrs Hepworth. Have you had a good day?	
Guest 2	Yes, thanks. Simon, can you recommend a good Indian restaurant?	
Simon	Well, the most famous one in the city is the Majestic on Bristol Street but **it gets very busy**. On Friday nights **you usually have to make reservations**.	
Guest 1	I see.	
Simon	But, in fact, **I think the Taj Mahal is better than the Majestic.** Also, it's cheaper. And **it's closer** too. **I'd recommend that.**	
Guest 2	Sounds good. Could you make reservations for us?	
Simon	**You don't usually need reservations.**	
Guest 1	OK, can you show us where it is on a map?	
Simon	Of course.	

Recommendations for places to eat | Unit 22

Later that evening

B

Simon	Hello, again. **How was your meal?**
Guest 2	Simon, thanks very much for your tip. It was an excellent recommendation. The food was great and the service was wonderful. And it was so cheap.
Simon	**I'm glad you liked it.**

Understanding

2 Listen to the conversations again and decide whether the statements are True or False.

1 The guests want to eat in an Indian restaurant. T / F
2 Simon thinks the Majestic is better than the Taj Mahal. T / F
3 Simon makes a table reservation for the guests. T / F
4 The Taj Mahal is more expensive than the Majestic. T / F
5 The guests were happy with Simon's recommendation. T / F

Key phrases	
Recommendations	
It gets very busy.	It's closer.
You usually have to make reservations.	I'd recommend that.
You don't usually need reservations.	How was your meal / evening?
I think restaurant X is better / cheaper than Y.	I'm glad you liked it.

Hotel & Hospitality English

Practice

3 Put the words in the sentences into the correct order.

1 your meal was How

_____?

2 glad you it I'm liked

_____.

3 reservations You need don't

_____.

4 busy The very restaurant gets

_____.

5 that I'd recommend

_____.

> ### Language tip
>
> Add *er* to one-syllable adjectives to make the comparative, for example, *close* → *closer*.
>
> With adjectives of two or more syllables, add *more*, for example, *expensive* → *more expensive*.

4 Use Simon's notes about local restaurants to compare the size and price of the restaurants and how popular they are.

1 Majestic Indian Restaurant [500 metres away]
Tables: 100; Dinner per person: £30–60; Reservation necessary? Always

2 Bella Roma Italian Restaurant [200 metres]
Tables: 30; Dinner per person: £20–40; Reservation necessary? Sometimes

3 Le Pont Bistro [1 kilometre]
Tables: 15; Dinner per person: £20–40; Reservation necessary? No

1 The Majestic is _____ than Bella Roma. (big)
2 Le Pont Bistro is _____ than the Majestic. (cheap)
3 Bella Roma is _____ than Le Pont Bistro. (expensive)
4 The Majestic is _____ than Le Pont Bistro. (popular)
5 Le Pont Bistro is _____ than Bella Roma. (small)
6 Bella Roma is _____ than the Majestic. (close)

Recommendations for places to eat | Unit 22

Speaking

> **Language tip**
>
> Use *I'd recommend* to give advice, for example, *I'd recommend the Taj Mahal* or *I'd recommend **going to** / **eating at** the Taj Mahal*.
>
> Use *I think* to give your opinion on something.

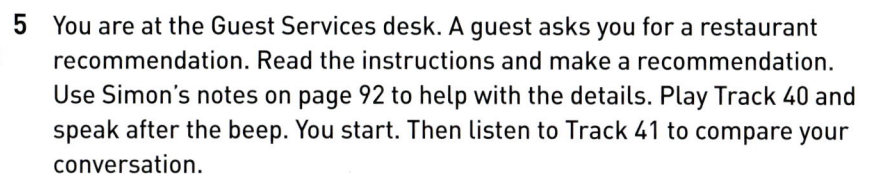

5 You are at the Guest Services desk. A guest asks you for a restaurant recommendation. Read the instructions and make a recommendation. Use Simon's notes on page 92 to help with the details. Play Track 40 and speak after the beep. You start. Then listen to Track 41 to compare your conversation.

You	(*Say hello to guest politely and ask what she wants.*)
Guest	Hi, my husband and I want to eat out tonight. Can you recommend a good restaurant?
You	(*Ask guest what kind of food she wants to eat.*)
Guest	We were thinking of Italian or French.
You	(*Use notes to give guest names of two restaurants.*)
Guest	Oh, that French one sounds interesting. Is it expensive?
You	(*Tell guest price range for dinner for two.*)
Guest	Wow. That sounds really cheap. Do we need reservations?
You	(*Tell guest that she won't have to reserve.*)
Guest	Great. I think we'll try it. Thanks for the recommendation.
You	(*Respond to guest's thanks and end conversation politely.*)

Now you can

Recommend a restaurant
Compare restaurants for guests
Ask if guests enjoyed their meal / evening

Hotel & Hospitality English | 93

23 Checking out

Checking guests out | Checking items on the bill | Saying goodbye

Conversation

1 Sarah is checking out a guest. Listen to her conversation.

Guest	Good morning. I'd like to check out, please.
Sarah	Good morning, sir. What was your room number?
Guest	Room 532.
Sarah	532 … Mr Smith. **How was your stay, Mr Smith?**
Guest	It was great, thank you.
Sarah	**Are you using the same credit card you gave me when you checked in?**
Guest	Yes, that's right.
Sarah	Fine, Mr Smith. **Please have a look at this printout:** two nights' accommodation, breakfast on Saturday and Sunday morning, bar drinks from Friday and last night, three phone calls and two newspapers.
Guest	Yes, that's all correct.
Sarah	**Did you have anything from the minibar last night?**

Hotel & Hospitality English

Guest	Oh yes, I almost forgot. We had two bottles of mineral water last night.
Sarah	OK. **I'll add those to your bill. Could you sign here, please?** Thank you. Would you like me to staple your credit card slip to your bill?
Guest	Yes, please. And here are our key cards.
Sarah	Thank you. There you are, Mr Smith. **See you next time. Have a safe trip home. Goodbye.**

Understanding

2 Listen to the conversation again and decide whether the statements are True or False.

1 Mr Smith is paying with a different credit card. T / F
2 Mr Smith stayed for two nights. T / F
3 Mr Smith didn't have anything from the minibar. T / F
4 Mr Smith didn't make any phone calls from his room. T / F
5 Mr Smith ordered a newspaper both mornings. T / F

Key phrases

Checking out

How was your stay?	*I'll add that / those to your bill.*
Are you using the same credit card (you gave me when you checked in)?	*Could you sign here, please?*
	See you next time.
Please have a look at this printout.	*Have a safe trip home.*
Did you have anything from the minibar?	

Practice

3 Put the words in the sentences into the correct order.

1 please here, you sign Could
   _____?

2 stay was How your
   _____?

3 have the you anything minibar Did from
   _____?

4 home safe trip Have a
   _____.

5 the card same you Are credit using
   _____?

4 Put the sentences into the correct order. The first one has been done for you. Listen to Track 43 to check your **answer**.

	Guest:	Yes, that's all correct.
	Sarah:	Did you enjoy your stay, Mrs Rand?
	Guest:	Yes, I did – I had a mineral water.
	Guest:	I was in Room 189. Mrs Rand.
1	Guest:	Good morning. Can I check out, please?
	Sarah:	OK. Please sign here and I'll staple the credit card slip to your bill.
	Sarah:	Thank you and see you again.
	Sarah:	Of course, madam. What was your room number?
	Guest:	Yes, it was very nice, thank you.
	Sarah:	Please take a look at this printout of your bill.
	Sarah:	Did you have anything from the minibar last night?
	Sarah:	See you again, madam. Have a safe drive home.

Speaking

5 Practise making questions using the past tense. Listen to Track 44 to compare your answers.

1. …. enjoy / stay?
   Your question: _____?
2. ….. what / room number?
   Your question: _____?
3. …. have / minibar / last night?
   Your question: _____?
4. … make / phone calls?
   Your question: _____?
5. …. use / pay TV?
   Your question: _____?

6 You are checking a guest out. Read the cues given and check out the guest. Play Track 45 and speak after the beep. Then listen to Track 46 to compare your conversation.

Guest	Hello. I'd like to check out, please.
You	(*Respond to request and ask for room number.*)
Guest	Room 631.
You	(*Give guest printout and ask him to check the bill.*)
Guest	That looks all correct.
You	(*Ask guest for credit card.*)
Guest	Here you are.
You	(*Ask guest for signature.*)
Guest	Of course. Could you staple my credit card slip to the bill, please?
You	(*Agree and give papers to guest.*)
Guest	Thank you.
You	(*Respond to guest's thanks and ask if everything was OK.*)
Guest	Yes, it was a great weekend. I'm sure we'll be back.
You	(*Wish guest safe trip and end conversation politely.*)

Now you can
- Check guests out
- Prepare the bill for a guest
- Say goodbye to guests

24 Problems checking out

Correcting mistakes on the bill | Apologizing | Keeping guests happy

Conversations

1 Sarah is checking out guests but there are a few problems. Listen to her conversations.

A	Guest	Excuse me, but this bill isn't correct. There are some incorrect charges on it.
	Sarah	**What's the problem, sir?**
	Guest	There are nine phone call charges but I never used the phone in my room. I used my own mobile phone!
	Sarah	I'm sorry, sir. I don't know how that happened! **I'll remove those and adjust your bill.**
	Guest	OK. Thank you.
	Sarah	I do apologize, sir. **Is everything else OK?**
	Guest	Yes. Everything else is fine. Thank you.

Problems checking out | Unit 24

B	Sarah	There you are, madam. Here's your credit card and your bill. **How was your stay?**
	Guest	Actually, not very good. It was very noisy last night and I couldn't sleep.
	Sarah	Oh, **I'm sorry to hear that, madam**. What caused the noise?
	Guest	There was a noisy group staying on my floor. They came back very late and woke me up.
	Sarah	Oh, my apologies. **I'll put a note in your file** and make sure you get a quieter room next time. **I'll also pass your comments on to our General Manager.**
	Guest	OK. Thank you. I know it wasn't your fault.
	Sarah	**I'm sure it won't happen next time you stay with us**, madam.

Understanding

2 Listen to the conversations again and answer these questions.

1. In conversation A, which charges does the guest question on his bill?
2. How does the guest know that the charges are incorrect?
3. In conversation B, why was the guest not happy?
4. What caused the problem in conversation B?
5. What does Sarah promise to do?

Key phrases

Checking out

What's the problem, sir / madam?	*I'll put a note in your file.*
I'll remove the charges.	*How was your stay?*
I'll adjust your bill.	*I'll pass your comments on to our General Manager.*
Is everything else ok?	
I'm sorry to hear that sir / madam.	*I'm sure it won't happen next time you stay with us.*

Practice

3 Use the verbs in the box to complete the sentences.

adjust   happen   hear   put   pass   remove

1 I'll _____ the incorrect call charges.
2 I'll _____ on your comments to the hotel manager.
3 I'm sure it won't _____ again, sir.
4 I'll _____ a note in your guest file.
5 I'm sorry to _____ that, madam.
6 I'll _____ your bill, sir.

4 Sarah passes on the guest's complaint and the General Manager later sends the guest an email. Complete the words in the email.

Dear Mrs Brown

I am s_____(1) to hear that your stay in our hotel last weekend wasn't completely satisfactory. I a_____(2) that you were disturbed late at night.

Next time you stay with us p_____(3) contact me directly and I will arrange for you to be upgraded to a s_____(4). Our suites are on a quiet f_____(5) and I am sure you w_____(6) be very comfortable.

I look forward to welcoming you back to the hotel soon.

Yours sincerely
Jim Heathcote
General Manager

Speaking

> **Language tip**
>
> When you use the verb *look forward to*, use the *ing* form, for example, *I look forward to **seeing** you again.*

5 Use the phrase *I look forward to* + *ing* to make statements to a regular guest.

1. see you again soon
   Your version: _____.
2. welcome you back to the Metro Hotel
   Your version: _____.
3. show you our new gym and swimming pool
   Your version: _____.
4. hear your thoughts on the new hotel design
   Your version: _____.
5. read your comments in our visitors book
   Your version: _____.

6 You are checking out a guest who has a problem with her bill. Read the cues given and check out the guest. Play Track 48 and speak after the beep. The guest starts. Then listen to Track 49 to compare your conversation.

Guest	Excuse me. There's a mistake on my bill.
You	(*Respond and ask for more information.*)
Guest	There's a charge for room service last night but I didn't order any room service.
You	(*Say sorry politely and tell guest you will change bill.*)
Guest	Thank you.
You	(*Show guest new changed bill. Ask if everything else is OK.*)
Guest	Thank you. Yes, everything else is correct.
You	(*Say sorry for mistake again and end conversation politely – so that guest will return.*)

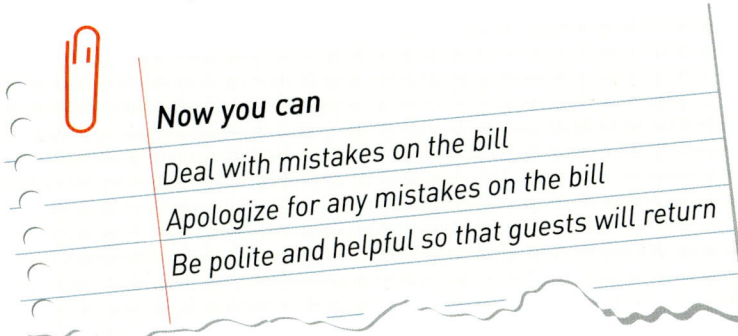

Now you can
Deal with mistakes on the bill
Apologize for any mistakes on the bill
Be polite and helpful so that guests will return

Answer key / Audio script

Unit 1

Conversation
1 See page 6 for audio script.

Understanding
2
1 Yes, she does.
2 She asks for a room on a lower floor.
3 Because she doesn't like using lifts.
4 She asks for a wake-up call at 6.30.
5 The hotel serves breakfast between 7.00 and 10.30.

Practice
3
1 Enjoy your stay.
2 Would you like a wake-up call?
3 Welcome to the hotel.
4 Breakfast is between 7.00 and 10.30.
5 Could I have your credit card, please?

4
1 Welcome
2 reservation
3 moment
4 floor
5 floor
6 have
7 credit
8 sign
9 wake-up
10 enjoy

Speaking
5
1 eleven thirty
2 seven o'clock
3 ten o'clock
4 twelve twenty
5 nine ten
6 five forty-five
7 nine fifty
8 one fifteen
9 three fifteen
10 two forty

6
Model conversation

You	Good afternoon. Welcome to the City Hotel.
Guest	Hello, my name's Yang. I have a reservation for one night.
You	Could I have your credit card?
Guest	Here's my VISA card.
You	Would you like a wake-up call?
Guest	Yes. I would like one at 6 o'clock tomorrow morning, please.
You	Good. 6 am. Would you like a newspaper?
Guest	Yes. Could I have a *Wall Street Journal*, please?
You	Yes, that's fine.
Guest	What time's breakfast?
You	Breakfast is between 7.00 and 10.30.

102 | Hotel & Hospitality English

Units 1–2

Unit 2

Conversation
1 See page 10 for audio script.

Understanding
2
1 False. It has been *delayed*.
2 True
3 False. It is £165 *including* breakfast.
4 True
5 True

Practice
3
1 Do you have a reservation?
2 I'm afraid so.
3 I can offer you our walk-up rate.
4 We're very busy this evening.

4
1 Surname
2 Street name
3 Post code
4 Nationality
5 Country code
6 Signature

Speaking
5
1 I'm afraid the hotel doesn't accept cheques.
2 I'm afraid we have no vacancies this evening.
3 I'm afraid you have to check out at noon.
4 I'm afraid that's the best rate I can offer you, sir.

6
Model conversation

1	
Guest	My room is very small. Can you upgrade it to a suite?
Reply	I'm afraid not.
2	
Guest	Do I really have to check out of my room by twelve o'clock?
Reply	I'm afraid so.
3	
Guest	Is the bar open now?
Reply	I'm afraid not.
4	
Guest	Is that charge for phone calls really correct?
Reply	I'm afraid so.

Answer key / Audio script

Unit 3

Conversation
1 See page 14 for audio script.

Understanding
2
1 Yes he does have a reservation.
2 He has arrived too early.
3 The usual check in time is 2 pm.
4 Sarah suggests he can store his luggage and go and have a cup of coffee.
5 He wants to freshen up and change before a meeting.

Practice
3
1 We would be glad to store your luggage while you are waiting.
2 May I suggest you have a drink in the bar while you are waiting?
3 I'm sorry, sir. Your room isn't quite ready yet.
4 When your room's ready, I'll come and get you.
5 Our normal check-in time is from 2 pm.
6 You're staying with us for two nights.
7 The coffee shop is just around the corner to your right.

4
1 Normally our check in time is from 2 pm.
2 You're welcome to store your luggage.
3 Your room isn't quite ready yet.
4 May I suggest you wait in the restaurant.
5 Housekeeping are still cleaning your room.
6 I'll come and get you when your room's ready.
7 I'm afraid your room isn't ready yet, sir.

Speaking
5
1 I'm sorry your room isn't ready yet, sir.
2 I'm sorry you are too early to check in, sir.
3 I'm sorry Housekeeping are still cleaning the rooms, madam.
4 I'm sorry I don't have any rooms ready at the moment.

6
Model conversation

You	Good morning. How can I help you?
Guest	Good morning. I have a reservation for tonight. My name's Jens Weiler.
You	Ah, yes. Mr Weiler.
Guest	When can I check in?
You	Our check in time is 2 pm, sir.
Guest	But I have a very heavy suitcase.
You	You're welcome to store your suitcase with us, sir.
Guest	And what should I do until my room is ready?
You	May I suggest you go for a cup of coffee in the coffee shop?
Guest	And where is the coffee shop?
You	Just go around the corner to your left, sir.

Units 3-4

Unit 4

Conversation
1 See page 18 for audio script.

Understanding
2
1 She has just checked in.
2 She needs to find an ATM / some local currency.
3 He didn't understand ATM.
4 Maple Street is five minutes' walk away.

Practice
3
1 catch
2 turn
3 map
4 pleasure
5 circle

4
1 left
2 right
3 left
4 right
5 left

Speaking
5
Model conversation

A	
Guest	Hello. My name is Monika Schl... . I have a meeting at 10 o'clock with one of your guests.
You	Sorry, I didn't quite catch your last name.

B	
Guest	I have to go to an office on R... Lane.
You	Sorry, I didn't quite catch the address.

C	
Guest	My booking reference is MH276... .
You	Sorry, I didn't quite catch the booking reference.

6
Model conversation

You	Good evening, madam. Can I help you?
Guest	I need to get to the train station. Can you tell me where it is?
You	Let me give you a map of the city. The hotel is here. I'll circle it for you.
Guest	Thank you very much.
You	The train station is about ten minutes' walk away.
Guest	OK.
You	So turn right out of the hotel. Walk along Green Street and turn left onto Madison Avenue. The train station is on your right.
Guest	That's very clear. Thank you very much.
You	You're welcome.

Answer key / Audio script

Unit 5

Conversations
1 See pages 22 and 23 for audio script.

Understanding
2
1 Mrs Hepworth wants Simon to order her a taxi.
2 She has to go to the Exhibition Centre.
3 She has to be there at 10 am.
4 Mr Smith wants to send a fax abroad.
5 Reception will help him.
6 It will cost 75 pence per page.

3
1 C   2 D   3 A   4 E   5 B

Practice
4

[1]	Guest	Hello? Jill Hepworth speaking.
[2]	Simon	Good morning, Mrs Hepworth. This is Simon from Guest Services.
[3]	Guest	Good morning.
[4]	Simon	I'm calling to let you know that your taxi has arrived.
[5]	Guest	Please tell the driver I'll be down in five minutes.
[6]	Simon	Very good, madam. I'll tell the taxi driver that you'll be here soon.

Speaking
5
Model conversation

A
You	Good morning, sir. Can I help you?
Guest	Yes. I have a question. Does the hotel have a swimming pool?
You	I'm sorry, sir. I'm afraid the hotel doesn't have a swimming pool.
Guest	Oh. What a pity. Never mind.
You	I'm sorry, sir.

B
You	Good morning, madam. How can I help you?
Guest	Hello. Could you order me a taxi for later, please?
You	Of course, madam. What time do you need the taxi?
Guest	I need it at noon.
You	OK, madam. I'll call your room when your taxi arrives.
Guest	Thank you.
You	You're welcome.

Units 5-6

Unit 6

Conversation
1 See page 26 for audio script.

Understanding
2
1 The caller wants to stay in the hotel on December 5th for 2 nights.
2 The room will cost £119 per night.
3 The price is for bed and breakfast.
4 The price is per room.
5 To guarantee the reservation.
6 The caller's credit card expires in March 2013.

Practice
3
1 Let me check.
2 I need it to guarantee the reservation.
3 Could you tell me the expiry date, please?
4 We look forward to seeing you in December.

4
1 five nine seven two – six double two six – two six seven two – three five zero eight
2 two seven double zero – six three six five – six seven five two – eight seven four eight
3 double two three seven – three four six three – seven three six two – seven four nine seven

Speaking
5
Model conversation

You	Good morning. Reservations.
Guest	Good morning. I'd like to reserve a single room for January 5th, please.
You	Let me check. Yes we have availability for January 5th.
Guest	How much will it cost?
You	I can offer you our best rate of £140 per night.
Guest	Does that include breakfast?
You	I'm afraid that is room only.
Guest	OK. I'll take it.
You	Could you please give me your name and credit card details?
Guest	It's Gardiner. J Gardiner. My VISA card number is 3-4-1-2 5-6-7-9 3-4-5-1 6-0-1-2, expiry date 10/14.
You	Thank you, Mr Gardiner. Your reservation number is M-H-4-3-5-X-Y. We look forward to seeing you in January. Goodbye.
Guest	Goodbye.

Answer key / Audio script

Unit 7

Conversations
1 See pages 30 and 31 for audio script.

Understanding
2
1 A change from two nights to three nights.
2 Yes, she can.
3 No, she doesn't.
4 48 hours.
5 By email.

Practice
3
1 confirmation
2 cancelled
3 reservation
4 there
5 charge
6 forward

4
1 January first
2 February second
3 March third
4 April fifth
5 May tenth
6 June sixteenth
7 July twentieth
8 August twenty-first
9 September twenty-second
10 October twenty-third
11 November thirtieth
12 December thirty-first

Speaking
5
Model conversation

You	Good morning. Metro Hotel.
Guest	Good morning. I need to cancel a reservation, please.
You	Could you tell me your reservation number, please?
Guest	The reservation number is M-F-2-6-4-F-K.
You	Mr Jackson on February twelfth?
Guest	Yes, that's correct.
You	That's fine. I've cancelled your reservation.
Guest	Will there be any charge?
You	No, there is no charge.
Guest	That's good. Can you send a confirmation email?
You	Of course. Thank you for your call. Goodbye.
Guest	Goodbye.

Unit 8

Conversations
1 See pages 34 and 35 for audio script.

Understanding
2
1 Call C
2 Call A
3 Call C
4 Call B

Practice
3
1 Please hold the line.
2 I'm afraid I can't give out our guests' room numbers.
3 I'll put you through to the restaurant now.
4 I'll send someone from Housekeeping up.
5 I'm very sorry about that.
6 Would you like to leave a message?

108 Hotel & Hospitality English

Units 7–8

4

[1]	Sarah	Good morning City Inn, Sarah speaking. How can I help you?
[2]	Mr Novak	Good morning. I'm calling to reconfirm a reservation but I've lost my reservation number.
[3]	Sarah	Hold the line, please. I'll put you through to Reservations.
[4]	Sarah	I'm sorry, Reservations seems to be busy. No one's answering. Could you give me your name?
[5]	Mr Novak	Yes, my name is Novak and I've reserved a double room for Saturday September 18th for two nights.
[6]	Sarah	Is that Mr Jan Novak?
[7]	Mr Novak	Yes, that's correct.
[8]	Sarah	Fine, Mr Novak. I've found your reservation. It is confirmed and your reservation number is MH434CW.
[9]	Mr Novak	Thank you.
[10]	Sarah	Thank you. Goodbye.

Speaking

5

1. one one two
2. six oh eight
3. two three one
4. eleven four two *or* one one four two
5. twelve oh six *or* one two oh six

6
Model conversation

A

You	Good morning, Sarah speaking.
Guest	I want to make a reservation, please.
You	I'll put you through to Reservations.
Guest	Thank you.
You	It's ringing for you now.

B

You	Good evening, Sarah speaking.
Guest	Hello. This is Mr Strong in Room two-oh-one. We need some more towels.
You	I'll ask Housekeeping to send some more towels to your room.
Guest	Thank you. How long will that take?
You	About five minutes.

C

You	Good afternoon, Sarah speaking.
Guest 1	Good afternoon. Can you give me Ian Diamond's room number, please?
You	I'm afraid I can't but I can put you through to his room.
Guest 1	Yes, please.
Guest 2	Hello, Ian Diamond speaking.

Answer key / Audio script

Unit 9

Conversations
1 See pages 38 and 39 for audio script.

Understanding
2
1 In call A, Sarah can't understand the caller because it is a bad line.
2 When he calls back, he wants to speak to a guest, Mr Diamond.
3 In call B, Sarah has problems with the guest's reservation number.
4 The correct last two letters of Mrs Harris' reservation number are JN.

Practice
3
1 Would you mind spelling your name for me?
2 Could you repeat that for me?
3 I'm sorry I didn't quite catch what you said.
4 Could you possibly call back?
5 One moment, I'll put you through.
6 Let me read that back to you.

4
1 Would you mind telling me your name?
2 Would you mind spelling that for me?
3 Would you mind repeating the last three numbers?
4 Would you mind calling back later?
5 Would you mind using a different phone?

Speaking
5
1 Omar Ali, Booking Reference M for Mike, H for Hotel, 9, 6, 5, P for Papa, W for Whisky
2 Gerry McDonnell, Booking Reference M for Mike, H for Hotel, 7, 3, 2, G for Golf, V for Victor
3 Tanya Koshkina, Booking Reference M for Mike, H for Hotel, 6, 4, 5, J for Juliet, Q for Quebec
4 Claire Birkel, Booking Reference M for Mike, H for Hotel, 1, 5, 2, S for Sierra, O for Oscar

6
Model conversation

You	Good morning Metro Hotel. How can I help you?
Guest	Good morning. My name is Mi... Wi.... I want to ... .
You	I'm sorry I didn't quite catch that. Would you mind repeating your name?
Guest	My name is Michelle ... .I want to ca... .
You	I'm sorry. I still can't understand. Could you possibly call back?
Guest	Hello. My name is Michelle Williams and I want to cancel a table for dinner.
You	That's much better, madam. One moment I'll put you through to the restaurant.
Guest	Thanks.
You	It's ringing for you.

Units 9–10

Unit 10

Conversations
1 See pages 42 and 43 for audio script.

Understanding
2
1 False. Room 855 smells of smoke; Room 1002 is the new room.
2 True
3 False. She tells her to wait in her room.
4 True
5 True

Practice
3
1 Please accept my apologies.
2 I'll send somebody up to collect your bags.
3 Would that be acceptable?
4 I can offer you a superior room.

4
1 accept
2 apologies
3 smoke
4 room
5 Thank you
6 superior
7 can

Speaking
5
Model conversation

You	Reception. Sarah speaking. How can I help you?
Guest	Hello. There is a problem with my room!
You	I'm very sorry to hear that. What's the problem?
Guest	I've just checked into Room 762 and I'm not happy. My room hasn't been cleaned. The bathroom is still dirty.
You	I'm very sorry about that.
Guest	Well? What are you going to do about it?
You	I can offer you a new room. Please wait in your room and I will send someone from Guest Services to collect your bags and move you to a new room.
Guest	OK. Thanks.

Now you call Guest Services.

Simon	Hello, Guest Services. Simon speaking.
You	Can you go up to Room 762 and move the guest to Room 1112?
Simon	OK.
You	Thanks.

Answer key / Audio script

Unit 11

Conversations
1 See pages 46 and 47 for audio script.

Understanding
2
1x coffee with milk
1x tea with milk
1x wholemeal toast
1x sausages, scrambled eggs, hash browns
1x blueberry pancakes

Practice
3
1 Feel free to help yourselves.
2 Please could I have your room number?
3 Can I bring you some coffee?
4 Would you like anything from the menu?
5 Enjoy your breakfast.

4
1 number
2 buffet
3 yourselves
4 menu
5 course
6 bring
7 away
8 coffee
9 would
10 breakfast

Speaking
5
Model conversation

You	Good morning, madam.
Guest	Good morning.
You	Could I have your room number, please?
Guest	I'm staying in Room 872.
You	Are you going to have the continental breakfast or something from the menu?
Guest	I haven't decided yet.
You	Here's the menu if you'd like to order something from the kitchen.
Guest	Thank you.
You	Would you like tea or coffee?
Guest	Could I have a pot of Earl Grey tea, please?
You	Would you like milk or lemon?
Guest	Lemon, please.
You	And can I bring you some toast?
Guest	Yes please. And I don't think I'll have anything from the menu.
You	Of course, madam. Feel free to help yourself to the buffet.
Guest	Thank you.
You	Here's your tea, madam. Enjoy your breakfast.

Hotel & Hospitality English

Units 11–12

Unit 12

Conversations
1 See pages 50 and 51 for audio script.

Understanding
2
1 False. He chooses a draught beer.
2 True
3 False. They ask for lots of ice and lemon.
4 False. They tell David a room number.
5 True. They want to start a tab.

Practice
3
1 What can I get you?
2 Shall I start a tab for you?
3 Would you like ice and lemon?
4 Would you like bottled or draught beer?

4

[1]	David	Good evening, sir. How are you this evening?
[2]	Guest	I'm, fine thank you.
[3]	David	What can I get you?
[4]	Guest	Scotch and soda, please.
[5]	David	Would you like ice?
[6]	Guest	No, thank you.
[7]	David	That'll be £6.00, please.
[8]	Guest	Can you charge it to my room?
[9]	David	Of course, sir. Can you give me your room number?
[10]	Guest	It's 1107.

Speaking
5
1 nine pounds ninety-nine or nine ninety-nine
2 three euros twenty or three twenty
3 eleven pounds fifty or eleven fifty
4 one hundred and forty-seven dollars ninety or one hundred and forty-seven ninety
5 sixteen euros forty-five or sixteen forty-five

6
Model conversation

You	Good evening, sir.
Guest	Good evening, how are you?
You	I'm fine, thank you. What can I get you?
Guest	I think I'll have a beer. What bottled beers do you have?
You	We have Grolsch, Heineken and Budweiser.
Guest	What would you recommend?
You	Well, Grolsch is very popular.
Guest	Fine. Then I'll have one of those.
You	Here you are, sir.
Guest	How much do I owe you?
You	That'll be four pounds.
Guest	Can I put it on a tab?
You	Of course, sir. Could you give me your room number?
Guest	I'm staying in Room 406.
You	Thank you sir. Could you sign here, please?

Answer key / Audio script

Unit 13

Conversations
1 See pages 54 and 55 for audio script.

Understanding
2
1 A mineral water with ice and lemon.
2 It is dirty and has lipstick around the edge.
3 It is the wrong kind of mineral water. She ordered still and has been given sparkling.
4 He thinks the bill is very high.
5 The service charge is 15%.

Practice
3
1 I'll take it back to the bar right away.
2 I'm afraid it's hotel policy.
3 I hope this one is better for you.
4 Is there a problem, madam?

4
1 with
2 to
3 at
4 to
5 on

Speaking
5
1 I am sorry that your food is cold, madam.
2 I do apologize for the wait, sir.
3 I am sorry that you don't like your table.
4 I do apologize for keeping you waiting.

6
Model conversation

Guest	Excuse me, waiter.
You	Yes, sir.
Guest	There's a problem with my drink.
You	What's the problem?
Guest	I asked for still water, not sparkling.
You	I do apologize, sir. I'll change if for you right away.
Guest	Thank you. Please be quick! I'm in a hurry.
You	I'll bring it right away.
Guest	Thank you.
You	Here's your water, sir. I'm sorry to have delayed you.
Guest	Thanks. That was quick.
You	I apologize again and hope you have a nice day.

Units 13–14

Unit 14

Conversation
1 See page 58 for audio script.

Understanding
2
1 Danielle offers to take their coats and bring them an aperitif.
2 They order prosecco.
3 No, she says that she will come back in a few moments.
4 The specials are rack of lamb, lemon sole or a vegetarian pasta dish.
5 Four house wines are on the wine list.

Practice
3
1 May I take your coats?
2 Can I bring you an aperitif?
3 Let me give you some menus.
4 Let me know when you are ready to order.
5 Would you like to see the wine list?
6 I'll come back to take your order in a few moments. / I'll come back in a few moments to take your order.

4
1 May I take your coat?
2 Good evening. Welcome to the restaurant.
3 Let me give you a menu.
4 Are you having wine this evening?
5 Let me know when you're ready to order.

5
1 E
2 D
3 A
4 B
5 C

Speaking
6
Model conversation

You	Good evening sir, good evening madam. Welcome to the Metro Restaurant.
Guest 1	Thank you. We have a table reserved for 8 pm in the name of Johansson.
You	Very good sir. May I take your coats?
Guest 2	Thank you. That's very kind.
You	Would you like an aperitif?
Guest 1	Yes please. I'll have a gin and tonic.
Guest 2	And I'd like a Campari and soda.
You	Let me give you two menus. I'll bring your aperitifs right away.
Guest 2	Thank you.
You	Would you like to see the wine list?
Guest 1	Yes, please.
You	Here's the wine list, sir.
Guest 2	The food all looks delicious. I'm very hungry. Are there any specials this evening?
You	Yes, madam. They're on the specials board behind you.
Guest 2	OK. I'll take a look.
You	I'll be back in a moment to take your orders.

Answer key / Audio script

Unit 15

Conversations
1 See page 62 for audio script.

Understanding
2
No appetizers

1x lemon sole
1x steak – cooked medium rare

1x bottle of house red
1x bottle of still water, 1x sparkling

Practice
3

[1]	Danielle	Good afternoon, madam. Are you ready to order?
[2]	Diner	Not quite. Please give me five more minutes
[3]	Danielle	Of course. I'll be back in a moment.
[4]	Danielle	Excuse me, I'm ready to order now.
[5]	Danielle	Very good, madam. What are you going to have?
[6]	Diner	I'll have pâté as an appetizer and then a Caesar salad with chicken, please.
[7]	Danielle	An excellent choice, madam. Are you going to have a glass of wine?
[8]	Diner	No, thank you. But could I have a bottle of water?
[9]	Danielle	Of course. Still or sparkling?
[10]	Diner	Still please, with ice and lemon.

4
1 Are you going to order some wine, sir?
2 Are you going to have an appetizer, madam?
3 Are you going to have a dessert?
4 What are you going to have for your main course?

Speaking
5
Model conversation

You	Good evening. Are you ready to order?
Guest 2	Yes, we are. Thank you.
You	What are you going to have, madam?
Guest 2	I'll start with the soup, please, and I'd like the mixed grill for my main course.
You	What are you going to have, sir?
Guest 1	I'd like oysters as an appetizer, please, and a seafood salad for my main course.
You	Are you going to have any wine?
Guest 2	Yes, please. A small glass of Shiraz.
Guest 1	And a large glass of Sauvignon Blanc.

116 | Hotel & Hospitality English

Units 15–16

You	Would you like any water?
Guest 2	Yes, please. A bottle of Perrier.
You	I'm afraid we don't serve Perrier. I'm sorry.
Guest 2	Oh, I see. What kinds of sparkling water do you have?
You	We have San Pellegrino, Voss, or Poland Spring.
Guest 2	Then we'll have a bottle of Poland Spring, please.
You	An excellent choice. I'll bring your drinks right away.

Unit 16

Conversation

1 See page 66 for audio script.

Understanding

2

1 No, they say that they will skip dessert.
2 Yes, they order two espressos.
3 The diner wants to pay by credit card.
4 The restaurant accepts Visa and MasterCard.
5 He wants to pay with a card which the restaurant doesn't accept.
6 1) put your card in the terminal,
  2) enter your PIN, and then
  3) press the green OK button.

Practice

3

1	May	4	afraid	7	enter
2	Was	5	accept	8	press
3	by	6	use		

Speaking

5

Model conversation

You	Have you finished with your meal?
Guest 1	Yes we have, thank you.
You	Was everything OK?
Guest 2	Yes, it was very good. My steak was perfectly cooked.
You	Thank you. Would you like to see the dessert menu?
Guest 1	No, thank you. I don't think we could eat anything else.
You	A coffee, perhaps?
Guest 2	Yes, please. Two espressos.
You	Would you like anything else?
Guest 1	No, thanks. Could I have our bill, please?
You	Of course. I'll bring the bill and your coffees right away.
Guest 1	Do you accept traveller's cheques?
You	I'm afraid we don't accept traveller's cheques. We only take cash or credit cards.
Guest 1	OK. Do you take AMEX?
You	Yes we do.
Guest 2	Is service included?
You	There's a 15% service charge added to the bill, sir. Here's the terminal. Put in your card, enter your PIN number then press OK.
Guest 1	Done. There you are.
You	Thank you, madam.

Hotel & Hospitality English

Answer key / Audio script

Unit 17

Conversation
1 See page 70 for audio script.

Understanding
2
1 There should be four hot drinks packets in the room every day.
2 Hot drinks packets are stored in the supplies cabinet on each floor.
3 There should be three toilet rolls in the bathroom at all times.
4 No. Sheets are only changed on the fourth day.
5 Yes. Pillowcases should be changed every day.

Practice
3
1 bathrobe
2 towels
3 bed
4 soap
5 toiletries
6 drinks packets
7 cups
8 toilet roll
9 safe

4
1 Make sure that you clean under the bed.
2 Don't forget to dust the mirror in the bedroom.
3 You must change the pillowcases every day.
4 You don't have to change the sheets every day.
5 Dust and polish all the surfaces.

5
1 You have to polish the TV.
2 You don't have to clean the windows.
3 You must replace the drinks packets.
4 You mustn't clean the TV screen with water.

Speaking
6
Model conversation

Maid	How often do I have to vacuum the room?
You	You must make sure you vacuum the room every day.
Maid	Even under the bed?
You	Yes, you must clean under the bed.
Maid	When do I change the sheets?
You	You only have to change the sheets every fourth morning.
Maid	And do I change the pillowcases every fourth day too?
You	No, you have to change the pillowcases every day.
Maid	How many coffee and tea packets do I put in the room?
You	Make sure you put two packets per person per day in the room.
Maid	Should I clean the TV screen with water?
You	No, you mustn't do that. Just use a duster.

Units 17–18

Unit 18

Conversations
1 See pages 74 and 75 for audio script.

Understanding
2
1 In conversation B.
2 In conversation A.
3 The room hasn't been cleaned; the breakfast dishes haven't been taken away; the bed hasn't been made; they need some fresh towels.
4 They aren't ready.
5 She asks him to hang the sign on the door when he is ready.

Practice
3
1 B
2 A
3 D
4 E
5 F
6 C

4
1 take
2 bring
3 take
4 bring

Speaking
5
Model conversation

You	Hello, Housekeeping. Karen speaking. How can I help you?
Guest	Good morning. We have a problem with our bed. Can you help?
You	Of course, madam. What's the problem?
Guest	My husband says the pillows are too soft. He says they hurt his neck.
You	I'll bring you some more pillows, madam. How many would you like?
Guest	That would be great. Could you bring six?
You	Certainly, madam. I'll bring you six extra pillows. What's your room number?
Guest	We're on the tenth floor in Suite 1023
You	I'll be up right away, madam.
Guest	Thank you very much.
You	You're welcome, madam. Thank you for calling.

6
Model conversation

You	Good morning, Housekeeping. I've come to clean your room.
Guest	Please don't come in. We're still in bed.
You	OK. Sorry to disturb you. I'll come back later.
Guest	Thank you.
You	Please hang the sign on the door when you want me to clean your room, sir.

Answer key / Audio script

Unit 19

Conversations
1 See pages 78 and 79 for audio script.

Understanding
2
1 She orders a continental breakfast.
2 She orders a cappuccino.
3 Her breakfast will be delivered in ten minutes.
4 She is in a hurry.

Practice
3

[1]	David	Room Service, can I help you?
[2]	Guest	Good morning. Can I order breakfast?
[3]	David	Of course, madam. What would you like?
[4]	Guest	I'd like a boiled egg with wholemeal toast and fresh fruit.
[5]	David	Very good, madam. Would you like tea or coffee?
[6]	Guest	Tea, please. English breakfast with milk.
[7]	David	Certainly, madam.
[8]	Guest	How long will that be? I have a meeting in an hour.
[9]	David	It'll be with you in 15 minutes.
[10]	Guest	Good.
[11]	David	Could I have your room number?
[12]	Guest	It's 745.
[13]	David	Thank you.

Speaking
4
Model conversation

You	Good evening. Room Service. David speaking. How can I help you?
Guest	Good evening. Is it too late to order some room service?
You	No, it isn't too late. What would you like?
Guest	Could I have a Metroburger with fries and a beer?
You	Of course. What kind of beer would you like?
Guest	I'll have a Budweiser, please.
You	Would you like ketchup with your burger?
Guest	Yes, please. How long will that be?
You	It'll be with you in 15 minutes.

5
Model conversation

Guest	Yes. What is it?
You	It's Room Service, sir. I've brought your order.
Guest	Oh, right. One moment, please.
You	Here's your burger, fries and beer, sir.
Guest	Just put it down on the table, please.
You	Of course, sir. Could you sign here, please?
Guest	Sure. Here you are.
You	Thank you, sir. Enjoy your food. Good night.

Units 19–20

Unit 20

Conversations
1 See pages 82 and 83 for audio script.

Understanding
2
1 False. The flowers are for her birthday.
2 True
3 True
4 False. He is flying at 13.50.
5 True

Practice
3
1 I'll just check for you.
2 Would you like me to look up something (or look something up) for you?
3 I'll take care of that for you.
4 I can make you an appointment if you like.

4
1 up
2 on
3 at
4 for
5 in
6 of

Speaking
5
Model conversation

You	Good morning. Can I help you?
Guest	Hello. Is there a sauna in the hotel?
You	Yes, there is.
Guest	Is it open at the weekend?
You	Yes, it is.
Guest	What time does it open today?
You	Today the sauna opens at 10 o'clock and closes at 8 o'clock this evening.
Guest	Is it a mixed sauna?
You	Yes, it is but it's ladies only on Saturday afternoon.
Guest	Thank you.
You	My pleasure. Have a nice day.

6
Model conversation

Guest	Can you look something up on the Internet for me?
You	Of course. What would you like me to look up for you?
Guest	Can you check which terminal the Delta flight from Toronto arrives at?
You	Certainly. I'll look it up right away.
Guest	Thanks.
You	The Delta flight from Toronto arrives in Terminal 5 at 20.15 this evening.
Guest	Thanks.
You	You're welcome. Have a nice day.

Answer key / Audio script

Unit 21

Conversations
1 See pages 86 and 87 for audio script.

Understanding
2
1 On the second floor.
2 No she doesn't because she's a guest.
3 Because her plug won't fit in the socket.
4 10 pence per page.
5 Yes, she can print in colour.

3
1 out
2 for
3 of
4 per
5 on
6 up

Speaking
4
Model conversation

You	Good morning. Can I help you?
Guest	Hi. Is this the business centre? I need to check my emails.
You	Yes it is, sir. Are you staying at the hotel?
Guest	Yes. I'm in Room 478.
You	The business centre is free for guests, sir.
Guest	Where can I plug in my laptop?
You	You can plug in your laptop in that socket over there.
Guest	Oh! My lead doesn't fit in this socket.
You	Would you like an adaptor, sir?
Guest	That would be great. Thanks a lot.
You	You're welcome.
Guest	Can I use the printer here too?
You	Yes, you can sir, but there is a charge.
Guest	How much does it cost?
You	It costs 10 pence per sheet.
Guest	Can I charge it to my room?
You	Yes, of course.

Units 21–22

Unit 22

Conversations
1 See pages 90 and 91 for audio script.

Understanding
2
1 True
2 False. Simon thinks the Taj Mahal is better.
3 False. You don't need reservations.
4 False. The Taj Mahal is cheaper.
5 True

Practice
3
1 How was your meal?
2 I'm glad you liked it.
3 You don't need reservations.
4 The restaurant gets very busy.
5 I'd recommend that.

4
1 The Majestic is *bigger* than the Bella Roma.
2 Le Pont Bistro is *cheaper* than The Majestic.
3 Bella Roma is *more expensive* than Le Pont Bistro.
4 The Majestic is *more popular* than Le Pont Bistro.
5 Le Pont Bistro is *smaller* than the Bella Roma.
6 Bella Roma is *closer* than the Majestic.

Speaking
5
Model conversation

You	Good evening, madam. How can I help you?
Guest	Hi, my husband and I want to eat out tonight. Can you recommend a good restaurant?
You	What kind of food do you want, madam?
Guest	We were thinking of Italian or French.
You	I'd recommend the Bella Roma Italian restaurant or Le Pont Bistro.
Guest	Oh, that French one sounds interesting. Is it expensive?
You	No. Dinner for two is twenty to forty pounds.
Guest	Wow. That sounds really cheap. Do we need reservations?
You	No, madam. You don't need reservations.
Guest	Great. I think we'll try it. Thanks for the recommendation.
You	You're welcome, madam. Enjoy your evening.

Answer key / Audio script

Unit 23

Conversation
1 See page 94 for audio script.

Understanding
2
1 False. He uses the same credit card.
2 True
3 False. He had two bottles of mineral water.
4 False. He made three phone calls.
5 True

Practice
3
1 Could you sign here, please?
2 How was your stay?
3 Did you have anything from the minibar?
4 Have a safe trip home.
5 Are you using the same credit card?

4

[1]	Guest	Good morning. Can I check out, please?
[2]	Sarah	Of course, madam. What was your room number?
[3]	Guest	I was in Room 189. Mrs Rand.
[4]	Sarah	Did you enjoy your stay, Mrs Rand?
[5]	Guest	Yes, it was very nice, thank you.
[6]	Sarah	Please take a look at this printout of your bill.
[7]	Guest	Yes, that's all correct.
[8]	Sarah	Did you have anything from the minibar last night?
[9]	Guest	Yes, I did – I had a mineral water.
[10]	Sarah	OK. Please sign here and I'll staple the credit card slip to your bill.
[11]	Guest	Thank you and see you again.
[12]	Sarah	See you again, madam. Have a safe drive home.

5
1 Did you enjoy your stay?
2 What was your room number?
3 Did you have anything from the minibar last night?
4 Did you make any phone calls?
5 Did you use the pay TV?

Speaking
6
Model conversation

Guest	Hello. I'd like to check out, please.
You	Of course, sir. What was your room number?
Guest	Room 631.
You	Please have a look at this printout, sir.
Guest	That looks all correct.
You	Could I have your credit card, sir?
Guest	Here you are.
You	Could you sign here, please?

Units 23–24

Guest	Of course. Could you staple my credit card slip to the bill, please?
You	Certainly, sir. Here you are.
Guest	Thank you.
You	You're welcome. Did you enjoy your stay?
Guest	Yes, it was a great weekend. I'm sure we'll be back.
You	We hope to see you again, sir. Have a safe trip.

Unit 24

Conversations
1 See pages 98 and 99 for audio script.

Understanding
2
1. In conversation A, the guest questions the telephone charges.
2. Because he used his own mobile phone and not the phone in his room.
3. Because she was woken up during the night.
4. Noisy guests on the floor were the problem.
5. Sarah promises to make a note in her file, pass on her comments to the General Manager and give her a quiet room next time.

Practice
3
1. remove   3. happen   5. hear
2. pass   4. make   6. adjust

4
1. sorry   3. please   5. floor
2. apologize 4. suite   6. will

5
1. I look forward to seeing you again soon.
2. I look forward to welcoming you back to the Metro Hotel.
3. I look forward to showing you our new gym and swimming pool.
4. I look forward to hearing your thoughts on the new hotel design.
5. I look forward to reading your comments in our visitors book.

Speaking
6
Model conversation

Guest	Excuse me. There's a mistake on my bill.
You	I'm sorry about that. What's the problem?
Guest	There's a charge for room service last night but I didn't order any room service.
You	I do apologize, madam. I'll remove the room service charge from your bill.
Guest	Thank you.
You	Here you are, madam, I've adjusted your bill. Is everything else OK?
Guest	Thank you. Yes, everything else is correct.
You	I apologize again, madam. We look forward to seeing you again soon.

Key phrases

Apologizing

I'm very sorry about that.
Sorry to disturb you.
Please accept my apologies.
I do apologize.
I'm afraid I can't do that.
I'm afraid not, sir.
I'm sorry it's closed now.

Asking for information

Do you have a reservation?
Can you tell me your name, please?

Asking someone to do something

Could you sign this, please?
Please could you give me your first name?
Can you tell me your room number, please?
Would you mind repeating that?
Please enter your PIN number.

Describing where things are

The business centre is on the first floor.
There's a swimming pool in the fitness centre.
There are two bars in the hotel.
The gift shop is next to the florist.
The continental breakfast is on the buffet over there.

Directions

Turn right, then take the first left, then go straight on.
Walk along the street.

Giving advice and recommending

Make sure you visit the museum.
The German and Czech pils on draught are very popular.
May I suggest you have a coffee in the restaurant?
I think the Taj Mahal is better than the Majestic restaurant.
I'd recommend the Taj Mahal.

Offering to do something

May I take your coats?

Let me take your bag.

Would you like me to take your orders now?

Shall I start a tab for you?

Polite instructions

Please hold the line.

Please put your card in the terminal, follow the instructions, enter your PIN, and then press the green OK button.

Enjoy your stay / breakfast.

Have a good day.

Saying what is necessary / not necessary

I need your credit card details to guarantee the booking.

You must check out by 12 noon.

You mustn't use bathroom towels at the swimming pool.

We have to clean the room now.

You don't have to pay extra for Wi-Fi. It's included in the room rate.

You don't need to make a reservation for the restaurant.

Saying what is possible / not possible

I can offer you a single room with shower.

I'm afraid I can't offer you a room with a bath.

Welcoming guests / Saying goodbye

Good morning / afternoon / evening.

Welcome to the Metro Hotel.

How are you today / this evening?

Have a nice day.

We look forward to seeing you again soon.

See you next time and have a safe trip home.

Goodbye.

Key words

Hotel personnel	
	Your translation
assistant manager	
bellboy (UK) / bellhop (US)	
concierge	
doorman	
duty manager	
food and beverages manager	
front-of-house manager	
general manager	
head waiter	
housekeeper	
maid / chambermaid (UK)	
meetings and conference manager	
night porter (UK) / doorman (US)	
porter (UK) / doorman (US)	
receptionist	
sales manager	
security guard	

Hotel departments, services and facilities	
	Your translation
ballroom	
bar	
business centre (UK) / business center (US)	
conference room	
florist	
gift shop	
guest services	
gym / fitness centre (UK) / fitness center (US)	
hairdresser	
housekeeping	
meeting room	
reception	
restaurant	
room service	
spa	
swimming pool	

Finding your way around the hotel	
	Your translation
corridor / hall (US)	
fire door	
fire escape	
lift (UK) / elevator (US)	
lobby	
reception	
revolving door	

Key words

Housekeeping and maintenance	
	Your translation
cloth	
duster	
furniture polish	
turn-down service	
vacuum cleaner / hoover (UK)	
to borrow	
to change the sheets / towels	
to clean a room	
to collect / deliver the dry-cleaning	
to dust	
to empty the bin	
to fix	
to inspect a room	
to iron	
to make the bed	
to mop	
to polish	
to repair	
to replace	
to replenish	
to restock	
to service a room	
to sweep	
to take away the room service tray	
to tidy	
to vacuum / to hoover (UK)	

Bookings, and checking in and out

	Your translation
accommodation	
advance purchase booking	
arrival date	
bed and breakfast	
bill	
cancellation deadline	
cancellation fee	
check-in / check-out time	
credit card guarantee	
departure date	
deposit	
full board (UK) / all meals included (US)	
half board (UK) / breakfast and dinner included (US)	
rack rate	
reception	
reservation	
room only	
walk-up rate	
to book (UK) / reserve a room	
to cancel a booking (UK) / reservation	
to change a booking (UK) / reservation	
to check in	
to check out	
to hold a booking (UK) / reservation	
to modify a booking (UK) / to change a reservation (US)	
to pay a bill	
to query a charge (UK) / to question a charge (US)	
to store luggage / baggage	

Key words

Hotel rooms	
	Your translation
alarm call (UK) / wake-up call	
alarm clock	
bed	
bedding	
blankets	
bunk beds	
cushion	
cot	
double bed	
double room	
duvet / quilt / comforter (US)	
duvet cover / comforter (US)	
foldaway bed	
king-size bed (UK) / king-sized bed (US)	
mattress	
pillow	
pillowcase	
queen size bed (UK) / queen-sized bed (US)	
sheet	
single bed (UK) / twin bed* (US)	
single room	
twin beds*	
twin room* (UK) / double room (US)	

* In American English, a small bed for one person is a *twin bed*. It can mean only one bed. In British English a *twin room* always has two single beds or *twin beds*.

Hotel room fixtures and fittings	
	Your translation
adaptor	
air conditioning	
blinds	
bottle opener / corkscrew	
coat hanger	
coffee and tea making facilities	
cupboard (UK) / cabinet / closet (US)	
curtains / drapes (US)	
Do not disturb / Please tidy my room sign	
docking station	
door chain	
drawers	
hairdryer (UK) / hair dryer (US)	
hotel services booklet / guide	
ice bucket	
iron	
ironing board	
laundry bag	
laundry list	
lock	
mini-bar	
note pad (UK) / notepad (US)	
pay TV	
plug	
radio	
remote control	
sachet (UK) / packet (US)	
safe	
slippers	
smoke alarm	
socket / power point (UK) / outlet (US)	
telephone	
television	
trouser press / pants press (US)	
TV channel / station	
video (UK) / movies on demand	
wardrobe	

Key words

Bathroom accessories	
	Your translation
cotton buds / Q-tips (US) / cotton swabs (US)	
dressing gown (UK) / bathrobe / robe	
feminine hygiene articles	
sewing kit	
shower cap	
toilet paper / bathroom tissue (US)	

Bathroom fixtures and fittings	
	Your translation
bathmat	
bath towel	
bathtub	
glasses	
hand towel	
hot tub	
jacuzzi	
mirror	
plug	
plughole (UK) / drain (US)	
shaving mirror	
shower	
shower curtain	
shower head	
shower screen	
shower tray	
sink / wash basin (UK)	
soap dish	
tap (UK) / faucet (US)	
toilet / lavatory (US)	
towel	
waste bin (UK) / wastebasket (US)	
waste bin liner (UK) / wastebasket liner (US)	

Bathroom toiletries	
	Your translation
conditioner	
razor	
shampoo	
shower gel	
soap	
toiletries	
toothbrush	
toothpaste	

Key words

Restaurant – on and around the table	
	Your translation
butter knife	
chair	
champagne flute	
crockery	
cup	
cutlery (UK) / flatware (US) / silverware (US)	
dessert bowl	
dessert menu	
dessert spoon	
fish knife	
fork	
jug (UK) / pitcher (US)	
knife	
menu	
napkin / serviette (UK)	
plate	
saucer	
side plate (UK) / bread plate (US)	
soup bowl / dish	
soup spoon (UK) / soupspoon (US)	
specials board	
spoon	
steak knife	
table	
table cloth	
teaspoon	
water glass	
wine / champagne bucket	
wine cooler	
wine glass	
wine list	

Restaurant and kitchen personnel	
	Your translation
busboy (US)	
chef	
head waiter	
maitre d'	
waiter	
waitress	
wine waiter (UK) / sommelier / wine steward (US)	

Restaurant – paying the bill	
	Your translation
bill (UK) / check (US)	
cover charge	
credit card terminal	
discretionary (especially UK) / optional	
service charge	
tip / gratuity	
to (leave a) tip	
to ask for the bill (UK) / check (US)	
to pay the bill (UK) / check (US)	
to bring the bill (UK) / check (US)	
to charge to a room	

Key words

Cooking methods	
	Your translation
baked	
barbecued	
basted	
blended	
boiled	
carved	
chilled	
chopped	
deep-fried	
diced	
dressed	
filled	
filleted	
frozen	
fried	
garnished	
grilled (UK) / broiled (US)	
marinated	
minced	
mixed	
poached	
poured	
roasted	
seasoned	
served	
shallow-fried (UK) / sautéd	
simmered	
sliced	
sprinkled	
steamed	
stewed	
stuffed	
whipped	
to taste	
to warm	
rare, medium-rare, medium, well done / medium well (US) [meat, usually beef]	
scrambled eggs, soft / hard boiled eggs	

Dining in the restaurant	
	Your translation
à la carte	
aperitif	
dessert / pudding (UK) / sweet (UK)	
digestif	
early bird menu	
first / second sitting	
fish course	
main course / entrée (US)	
set / fixed price menu	
starter (UK) / appetizer	
table d'hôte / prix fixe (US)	
two- / three- / four-course meal	
to book / reserve a table (UK) / to make a reservation (US)	
to cancel a booking / reservation (US)	
to clear a table	
to complain about the food	
to confirm a booking / reservation (US)	
to order	
to seat somebody	
to (ask to) see the menu	
to show somebody to a table	

Key words

In the bar	
	Your translation
bar	
bar stool	
barkeeper (UK)	
barman (UK) / barmaid (UK) / bartender (US)	
beer mat / coaster	
bottle opener	
bottle top	
cocktail shaker	
cork	
corkscrew	
crushed ice	
happy hour	
ice (cube)	
measure	
on tap (US) / draught (UK) / draft (US)	
snacks	
to mix a drink / cocktail	
to open a bottle	
to order a drink	
to pour	
to serve	

Alcoholic drinks

	Your translation
Beer	
bottled beer	
draught beer (UK) / draft beer (US)	
lager	
light beer	
wheat beer	
Wine	
white wine	
dry white wine	
medium dry white wine	
sweet white wine	
red wine	
rosé wine	
dessert wine	
sparkling wine	
Other	
cocktail	
double measure	
measure	
short	
spirits	

Non-alcoholic drinks

	Your translation
coffee	
fizzy (UK) / sparkling	
mineral water	
mixers	
non-alcoholic beer	
slice of lemon	
soda water	
soft drinks	
still water	
tap water (UK)	
tea	

Grammar reference

Present simple

Words that often take the present simple are: *often, seldom, usually, never, always, normally, rarely:*

- It **often** rains a lot in April.
- We **never** close.

Positive forms:	I **work** on the reception desk. She **enjoys** her job very much. Our employees **love** helping guests.
Negative forms:	I **don't [do not] work** for the Savoy Hotel. This guest **doesn't [does not] have** a reservation. We **don't allow** dogs in the restaurant.
Questions:	**Does** she **work** for the Metro Hotel? Where **do** you **come** from?
Long answers:	Yes, she **does work** for the Metro Hotel. No, she **doesn't work** for the Metro Hotel.
Short answers:	Yes, I **do**. No, I **don't**. Yes, she **does**. No, she **doesn't**.

This tense is used to express facts:

- Chris **works** in London but he **comes** from the USA.
- Kate **works** in a hotel in Manchester and she **lives** in Liverpool.
- The hotel **is** on the corner of Market Street and East Parade.

and for actions that are regular activities or routines:

- We **clean** the rooms every day.
- The senior housekeeper **checks** the rooms after they are serviced.

It is also used with timetables and schedules:

- The hotel swimming pool **opens** at ten o'clock.
- The hotel bar **closes** at midnight.

It is also used in clauses with *if*, *when*, *until*, *as soon as* and *after*:

- She'll give you her credit card *when* she **checks in**.
- I'll help you *after* I **finish** this room inspection.
- We'll start the meeting *as soon as* the duty manager **arrives**.
- Let's wait *until* the General Manager **gets here**.

Present continuous

Words that often take the present continuous are: *now, at the moment, presently*.

Positive form:	I'm [I am] **waiting** for my bill.
	We're [We are] **staying** in Room 641
	They're [They are] **celebrating** their wedding anniversary
Negative form:	No, I'm not **staying** in the hotel
	She **isn't** [She **is not**] **queuing** for breakfast.
Questions:	**Are** you **staying** in the hotel?
	Is Mr Jones **waiting** to check in?
	When **are** they **leaving**?
Long answers:	Yes. I'm **staying** in the hotel.
	No, I'm **not** staying in the hotel.
Short answers:	Yes, I **am**.
	No, I'm **not**.
	Yes, she **is**.
	No, she **isn't**.
	Yes, they **are**.
	No, they **aren't**.

This tense is used to describe an action that is happening now:

- Would you like an umbrella because it's **raining** (now)?

Or an action that has started but is not finished:

- I'm **waiting** to check in.

It is also used for temporary actions or situations:

- She's **staying** at the Metro Hotel in New York for three nights.

It can also have a future meaning and is used to talk about future activities that have been arranged or planned:

- I'm **staying** in the hotel next week too.

> **Watch out – we don't usually use these verbs in the continuous form:**
> remember, understand, want, like, belong, suppose, need, seem, prefer, believe, know, think (= believe), hear, smell, have (= possess)

Grammar reference

Past simple

Words that often take the past simple are: *yesterday, an hour ago, last year, in 2009, last week, a year ago*.

Positive form:	He **checked** in yesterday. I **confirmed** my booking last week. We **refurbished** all the suites last month. She **knew** there was a cancellation fee. We **ate** in the restaurant last night.
Negative form:	He **didn't (did not) check in** yesterday. She **didn't tell** me that I would have to pay. They **didn't enjoy** their breakfast. I **didn't expect** to have to wait so long for a table.
Questions:	**Did** Mr Lawson **check in** yesterday? **Did** you **enjoy** your stay ladies? **Did** the guests **receive** a wake-up call this morning? What **did** you **have** from the mini-bar?
Long answers:	Yes, he **checked in** yesterday. No, he **didn't check in** yesterday. Yes, we **spoke** to the manager about your complaint. No, **we didn't speak** to the manager about your complaint.
Short answers:	Yes, we **did**. No, we **didn't**. Yes, I **did**. No, I **didn't**.

This tense is used for finished actions in the past:

- I **stayed** at your hotel last week.

and for longer situations in the past:

- I **worked** at the Raffles Hotel for 20 years.

Going to future

Positive form:	I'm [I am] going to check out tomorrow. They're [They are] going to complain about the service. He's [He is] going to book three conference rooms. We're going to write to the manager.
Negative form:	I'm not [I am not] going to check out tomorrow. We aren't [We are not] going to eat in the hotel after all. She isn't [is not] going to take the room on the ground floor.
Questions:	Are you going to check out tomorrow? Is he going to make a complaint? Who's going to clean Room 101?
Long answers:	Yes, I'm going to check out tomorrow. No, I'm not going to check out tomorrow. Yes, they're going to write to the manager. No, they aren't going to write to the manager.
Short answers:	Yes, I am. No, I'm not. Yes, he is. No, he isn't. Yes, they are. No, they aren't.

This tense is used to say that something has been planned or decided and will definitely happen:

- What are you going to order?
- We're going to refurbish the hotel next year.
- When are you going to clean room 234?
- When I get home, I'm going to write a review on the hotel.

Grammar reference

Simple future – will

Positive form:	I**'ll** [I **will**] **post** it tomorrow. We**'ll do** our best, sir. They**'ll call** me as soon as your room is ready, madam.
Negative form:	I **won't** [**will not**] **do** it tomorrow. George **won't forget** to do it, madam. They **won't come** back.
Questions:	**Will** you **do** it tomorrow? **Will** they **call** my room when my dry cleaning is ready? When **will** my room **be** ready?
Long answers:	Yes, I**'ll do** it in a minute. No, I **won't do** it tomorrow.
Short answers:	Yes, I **will**. No, I **won't**.

This tense is used to announce spontaneous decisions, offers, promises, requests, instructions and suggestions:

- I'll send someone up to clean the room.
- That sounds good. I**'ll have** the steak too.
- The room **won't be** ready until 2 pm.
- I**'ll tell** you as soon as your room is ready.
- **Will** you **fill** in this form please?

Present perfect simple

Positive form:	I**'ve** [I **have**] **worked** here for 10 years. She**'s** [She **has**] **done** bar work before. They**'ve stopped** serving breakfast now. The manager **has read** your letter.
Negative form:	I **haven't** [**have not**] **worked** in a hotel before. She **hasn't** [**has not**] **cleaned** the bathroom.
Questions:	**Have** you **worked** in a hotel before? **Has** my room **been** serviced? Where **have** you **put** the keys?
Long answers:	Yes, I**'ve finished** the rooms on the fifth floor. No, I **haven't** [**have not**] **seen** a mobile phone in the corridor.
Short answers:	Yes, I **have**. No, I **haven't**. Yes, it **has**. No, it **hasn't**.

This tense is used to describe a completed action in the past which is still relevant to the present.

- Can you help me? I**'ve lost** my room key. (= I don't have it)
- We have to cancel our booking because she's **broken** her leg. (= Her leg is broken)
- I**'ve read** some good reviews of your hotel. (= I know about the hotel)
- We**'ve renovated** all the rooms since your last stay. (= The rooms are now renovated)

> Note that we **do not** use the present perfect if we say when something happened, for example, with finished time expressions such as *yesterday, last week, at ten o'clock this morning, in 2010, last October*.

- I'm sure we**'ve met** before!
- **Have** you ever **stayed** in the hotel before?
- The hotel **has been** in the Metro Group for over 25 years.

It is also used to describe events with expressions of 'time elapsing up to now'. Signal words are *just, yet, already*.

- **Have you serviced** Room 1010 **yet**?
- She**'s just finished** the rooms on the sixth floor.
- We**'ve just received** a cancellation.
- I**'ve already ordered** Mrs Wilson's flowers.

Grammar reference

Comparatives and superlatives

When we compare two things, we add the suffix -er to the adjective and use the word *than*. When we compare more than two things, we add the suffix -est to the adjective.

adjective	comparative	superlative
small	smaller than	the smallest
big	bigger than	the biggest
cheap	cheaper than	the cheapest
high	higher than	the highest

- Your hotel room is **smaller than** mine.
- The Metro Hotel is **bigger than** the Travelstay Hotel.
- The Ritz is **the biggest** hotel in the city.
- Our **cheapest** room is £49 per night.
- The 14th floor is **the highest** floor in the hotel.

If an adjective has two or three syllables, for example, *ex-pen-sive*, then we don't add -er. In the comparative we use the words *more* or *less* before the adjective. We don't say ~~expensiver than~~ or ~~difficulter than~~. In the superlative we use the words *most* or *least*.

adjective	comparative	superlative
expensive	more / less expensive than	the most / least expensive
beautiful	more / less beautiful than	the most / least beautiful
difficult	more / less difficult than	the most / least difficult
exclusive	more / less exclusive than	the most / least exclusive

- The Carlton Hotel is **more expensive than** the Metro.
- The view from our rooftop restaurant is the **most beautiful** in the city.
- The Presidential Suite is the **most exclusive** room we have, sir.
- He was one of the **most difficult** guests I have ever served.

Two-syllable adjectives ending in –y, for example *pretty*, follow the one syllable adjective comparative and superlative forms.

- The Royal Park is **prettier than** the City Gardens. In fact, it is **the prettiest** place to walk in the city.

Hotel & Hospitality English

If we are saying things are the same or not the same then we use (*not*) *as ... as*.

adjective	comparative
big	as big as
beautiful	as beautiful as
expensive	as expensive as
cheap	as cheap as
good	as good as

- The food in the bistro is *as tasty as* the food in the restaurant.
- The bistro is *not as expensive as* the restaurant.
- A club room is *not as big as* a superior room.
- The Metro Hotel is just *as cheap as* the Grand Hotel.
- The service here is *just as good as* the service in the Grand Hotel.

Note that the words ~~gooder~~ and ~~goodest~~ and ~~badder~~ and ~~baddest~~ don't exist but have irregular forms.

adjective	comparative	superlative
good	better	best
bad	worse	worst

- This hotel is *better than* the last one we stayed in.
- This is *the best* steak I've ever tasted.
- The service is much *worse than* it was last year.
- I think this is *the worst* customer feedback I have ever read.

Model emails

Confirming a reservation (1)

Confirmation Number: 80139942

Dear Mr Jones

We are pleased to confirm your reservation with the Metro Hotel.

Reservation Details
Confirmation Number: 80139942
Your hotel: Metro Hotel
Check-in: Thursday 5 May 2012 (16:00)
Check-out: Friday 6 May 2012 (12:00)
Room type: King room
Number of rooms: 1
Guests per room: 2
Guest name: Robert Jones
Reservation confirmed: Thursday 3 March 2012

Guarantee method: Credit card guarantee

Summary of Room Charges
Thursday 5 May 2012 - Friday 6 May 2012: 1 night
Cost per night per room - GBP 270.00
Stay for Breakfast rate, includes breakfast for 2 adults
Estimated government taxes and fees - GBP 54.00

Total for stay (for all rooms) - GBP 324.00

Cancelling Your Reservation
You may cancel your reservation for no charge until 16:00 hotel time on Thursday 5 May 2012.
Please note that we will charge a fee of GBP 324.00 if you cancel after this deadline.

We look forward to welcoming you to the Metro Hotel.

Yours sincerely

J. Smith
Reservations Manager

Confirming a reservation (2)

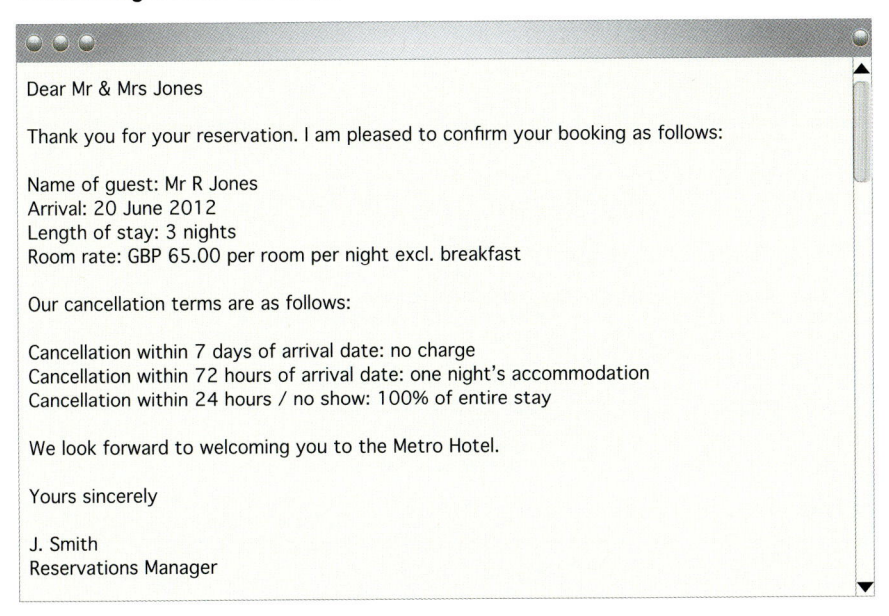

Dear Mr & Mrs Jones

Thank you for your reservation. I am pleased to confirm your booking as follows:

Name of guest: Mr R Jones
Arrival: 20 June 2012
Length of stay: 3 nights
Room rate: GBP 65.00 per room per night excl. breakfast

Our cancellation terms are as follows:

Cancellation within 7 days of arrival date: no charge
Cancellation within 72 hours of arrival date: one night's accommodation
Cancellation within 24 hours / no show: 100% of entire stay

We look forward to welcoming you to the Metro Hotel.

Yours sincerely

J. Smith
Reservations Manager

Confirming a cancellation

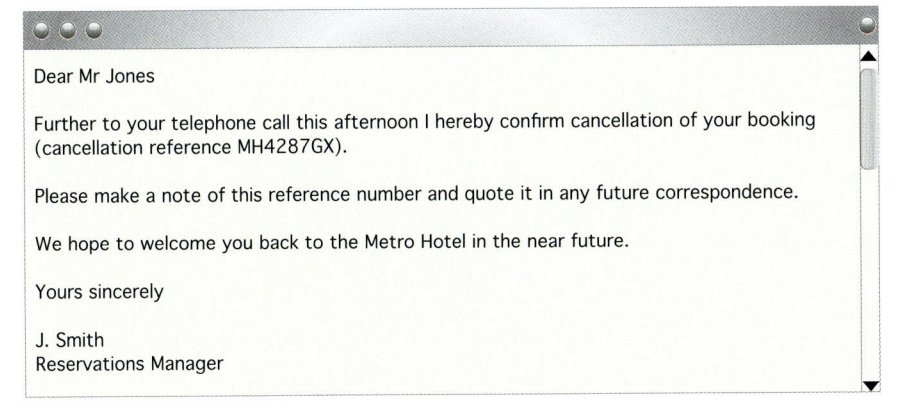

Dear Mr Jones

Further to your telephone call this afternoon I hereby confirm cancellation of your booking (cancellation reference MH4287GX).

Please make a note of this reference number and quote it in any future correspondence.

We hope to welcome you back to the Metro Hotel in the near future.

Yours sincerely

J. Smith
Reservations Manager

Model emails

Replying to an inquiry

Dear Mr & Mrs Jones

Thank you for your inquiry. For the dates you requested I can quote you the following rates:

Advance Purchase Rate: GBP 85 per room per night room only*
Advance Purchase Rate: GBP 95 per room per night bed and breakfast*

*Please note that these rates are payable at the time of booking and are non-refundable.

Standard Rate: GBP 100 per room per night room only
Standard Rate: GBP 115 per room per night bed and breakfast

Weekend Rate: GBP 205 per room bed and breakfast**

**NB: Only valid for Saturday and Sunday nights.

Please do not hesitate to contact me if you require any further information.

We look forward to welcoming you to the Metro Hotel.

Yours sincerely

J. Smith
Reservations Manager

Responding to positive feedback

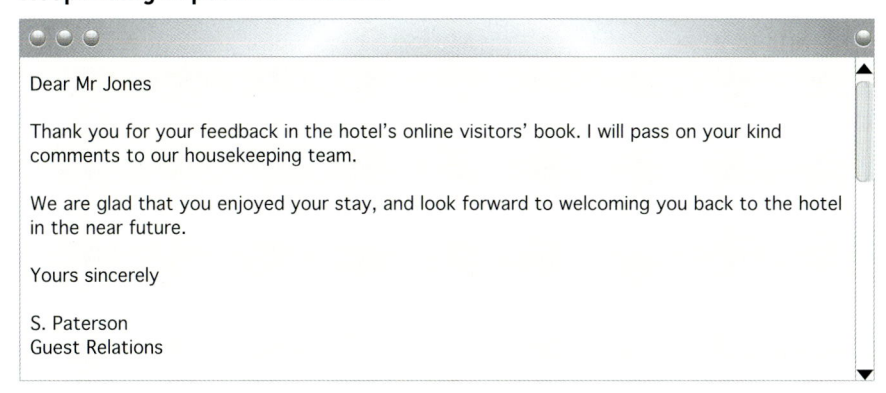

Dear Mr Jones

Thank you for your feedback in the hotel's online visitors' book. I will pass on your kind comments to our housekeeping team.

We are glad that you enjoyed your stay, and look forward to welcoming you back to the hotel in the near future.

Yours sincerely

S. Paterson
Guest Relations

Responding to negative feedback

Dear Mr Jones

Thank you for your recent feedback on your stay in June. I am sorry that this stay did not live up to your expectations. I have passed on your comments to my team and they will address all the issues you raised.

I hope this experience will not stop you staying with us in the future. When you next return to the hotel please contact me directly on [phone number] and I will arrange for you to be upgraded to a superior room.

Yours sincerely

P. Doyle
General Manager

How do I say ... ?

Dates	
You write	You say
Monday 18 August (especially UK)	Monday, the eighteenth of August
Monday, August 18 (US)	Monday, August (the) eighteenth
2011	two thousand and eleven **OR** twenty eleven
2/11/2011 (UK)	the second of November, two thousand and eleven **OR** twenty eleven
11/2/2011 (US)	November the second, two thousand and eleven **OR** twenty eleven
October 3rd (US)	October (the) third
3rd October (UK)	the third of October

- In British English you usually write and say dates like this: date / month / year.
- In American English you usually write and say dates like this: month / date / year.

Times	
The time is....	You say
09.15	nine fifteen **OR** quarter past nine **OR** quarter after nine (US)
10.00	ten o'clock (in the morning) **OR** ten am
22.00 (UK)	ten o'clock (in the evening) **OR** ten pm
11.30	eleven thirty **OR** half past eleven
14.40	fourteen forty (UK) **OR** two forty in the afternoon **OR** twenty to three
16.20	sixteen twenty **OR** twenty past four (in the afternoon) **OR** twenty after four (US)
16.21	sixteen twenty one **OR** twenty one **minutes** past four
15.00	fifteen hundred (hours) **OR** three o'clock (in the afternoon)
17.45	seventeen forty-five **OR** quarter to six

- In American English you don't use the 24-hour clock. For example, 22.00 is 10 pm and 10.00 is 10 am.

Periods of time	
1.5 hours	ninety minutes **OR** one and a half hours **OR** an hour and a half
15 minutes	fifteen minutes **OR** quarter of an hour
30 minutes	thirty minutes **OR** half an hour
45 minutes	forty five minutes **OR** three quarters of an hour

- In British English you use the 24-hour clock (16.45 = sixteen forty five) mainly when we talk about train and flight times. The 24-hour clock is rarely used in American English.
- We don't usually use the 24-hour clock (16.45 = sixteen forty five) in everyday language. For example, we do not say ~~Your room will be available at fifteen hundred hours~~ but do say *Your room will be available at three pm / at three o'clock.*

Prices	
You write	**You say**
£10.99	ten pounds ninety-nine (pence)
€140.00	one hundred (and) forty euros
$22.90	twenty two (dollars) (and) ninety (cents)
£87.00	eighty seven pounds

Telephone numbers	
The telephone number is:	**You say:**
0044 171 200 3612	double oh, double four, one seven one, two double oh, three six one two (UK)
0044 171 200 3612	zero zero four four, one seven one, two zero zero, three six one two (US)
020 677 3219	oh two oh six double seven, three two one nine
ex: 5640	extension five six four oh (UK)
ex: 5640	extension five six four zero /oh (US)

- In American English you don't usually say *double four* or *treble four*. Just say *four four*, or *four, four, four*.
- You can say *oh* or *zero* for the number 0. *Zero* is used more often in American English.

Hotel room numbers	
The room number is:	**You say:**
Room 101	Room one oh one
Room 370	Room three seven oh / three seven zero
Room 1021	Room one oh two one / Room ten twenty-one / Room ten two one

Hotel room sizes	
How big is the room?	**You say:**
7 m × 8 m	seven metres **by** eight metres
22 ft × 12 ft	twenty-two feet **by** twelve feet
38m²	thirty-eight square metres

On the phone – useful phrases

You can use these phrases when you're on the phone. Why don't you photocopy these 2 pages and keep them near the telephone for easy reference.

Asking to speak to someone on the phone

50 CD2

- Could I speak to _____, please?
- Can I speak to _____, please?
- Could you put me through to _____, please?
- I'm trying to contact _____.
- I'm trying to get in touch with _____.
- I'm trying to get hold of _____.

Asking for identification on the phone

51 CD2

- Who's calling, please?
- Who's speaking?
- Who shall I say is calling?
- Could I have your name (again), please?
- Could you give me your name, please?
- I'm sorry I didn't quite catch / get your name.
- **Would you mind** spell**ing** that (your name / first name / surname) for me?
- Could you spell that for me?

Asking for repetition / clarification on the phone

52 CD2

- I'm sorry, I didn't quite catch / get that. Could you repeat it?
- I'm afraid that was a little (bit) too fast. **Would you mind** repeat**ing** it more slowly for me?
- I didn't understand the last word of the address. Could you give it to me again?
- Is that Mr Cerales or Mrs?
- I'm sorry, did you say Oxford Road or Oxford Parade?
- Pardon? / I beg your pardon?
- Sorry?
- I'm (very) sorry. I'm not familiar with English / French / Japanese surnames. Could you spell that for me?
- Could you repeat that a little more slowly, please?

You may photocopy these pages.

Hotel & Hospitality English

Keep next to your phone for easy reference

Asking the caller to wait

- Hold the line, please.
- Please hold the line.
- Would you (just) hold the line a moment, please?
- (Just) One moment, please. I'm just putting you through to that room / department.
- Could you hold on a moment, please?
- Could you wait a moment, please?
- One moment, please. I'll be with you in a second.

Answering the phone

- Good morning, Metro Hotel. Simon speaking. How can I help you?
- Good morning, Metro Hotel. Simon speaking. How may I direct your call?

Offering to help

- I'm sorry, the line's busy. Can I help?
- I'm sorry, the number's engaged. Can I help?
- I'm sorry, there's no one answering. Can I take a message?
- Would you like to leave a message?

The aviation alphabet

Use the following words to check spelling.

My name's Mr Whyte- that's W for Whisky, H for Hotel, Y for Yankee, T for Tango and E for Echo.

A for Alpha	G for Golf	M for Mike	S for Sierra	Y for Yankee
B for Bravo	H for Hotel	N for November	T for Tango	Z for Zulu
C for Charlie	I for India	O for Oscar	U for Uniform	
D for Delta	J for Juliet	P for Papa	V for Victor	
E for Echo	K for Kilo	Q for Quebec	W for Whisky	
F for Foxtrot	L for Lima	R for Romeo	X for X-Ray	

Note that Z is pronounced *zee* in American English and *zed* in British English.

You may photocopy these pages.

Hotel & Hospitality English

Notes

Notes

Photographs in *Hotel & Hospitality English* were taken on location at Mint Hotel.

HarperCollins would like to thank Mint Hotel for their kind co-operation on this project.

minthotel

Mint Hotel presents guests with a fresh, contemporary hotel experience, where a commitment to innovation and putting customers first remains at the heart of the brand's values. That's why you'll find floor-to-ceiling windows and an Apple iMac in each guest room, modern meeting rooms with natural daylight, free Wi-Fi throughout our hotels and vibrant destination bars and restaurants with outside spaces to make the most of the city-centre locations.

Mint Hotel is now in eight thriving cities where business, education, arts and culture are all at the heart of a distinguished civic tradition – In the UK in Birmingham, Bristol, Glasgow, Leeds and Manchester, in central London at Westminster and at the Tower of London, and most recently in Amsterdam, The Netherlands.

Mint Hotel is delighted to have been involved with the production of this book.

www.minthotel.com

Dados Internacionais de Catalogação na Publicação (CIP)
(Câmara Brasileira do Livro, SP, Brasil)

Seymour, Mike
    Hotel & Hospitality English / Mike Seymour. – São Paulo : Editora WMF Martins Fontes ; London : HarperCollins, 2012.

    ISBN 978-85-7827-490-0

    1. Inglês - Estudo e ensino I. Título.

11-12839   CDD-420.7

Índices para catálogo sistemático:
1. Inglês : Estudo e ensino 420.7